The Juaneño-Acjachema

Exploring Identity and the Reproduction of Culture

Candace Coffman

Kendall Hunt
publishing company

Front Cover image provided by the author.
Back Cover image © Shutterstock, Inc. Used under license.

Kendall Hunt
publishing company

www.kendallhunt.com
Send all inquiries to:
4050 Westmark Drive
Dubuque, IA 52004-1840

Copyright © 2012 by Candace Coffman

ISBN 978-0-7575-9693-3

Printed in the United States of America
10 9 8 7 6 5 4 3 2 1

contents

Chapter 1

INTRODUCTION 1

Chapter 2

JUANEÑO–ACJACHEMA HISTORY AND CULTURE........17

Chapter 3

THE JUANEÑO-ACJACHEMA TODAY 41

Chapter 4

THE REPRODUCTION OF PEOPLE AND CULTURE......77

Chapter 5

CONCLUSION 109

APPENDIX 1 133
APPENDIX 2 137
APPENDIX 3 143
REFERENCES 145

chapter 1

Introduction

Ancestor's Walk 2003

Panhe, San Mateo Campground, just outside of San Clemente, California. It is just past 7:30 am. It is cold, misty. A group of fifty gathers. Some of the women are in skirts; all are bundled in coats. The people here today are Juaneño-Acjachema, Luiseño, Gabrieleño-Tongva, Chumash, and non-Indians like myself. I am attending the event with my daughter Cassandra, who is nine years old. Sage is being burned. Some Juaneño women have their clappers; a few men have rattles.[1] We circle up. The elder leading the walk, a man of mixed Juaneño-Acjachema and Gabrieleño-Tongva heritage, Jimi Castillo, talks about the purpose of this event. We are here to honor the ancestors of the Juaneño-Acjachema and Gabrieleño-Tongva people. The sites to be visited today are all burial sites, village sites, or sacred sites; some are sites of the reburials of remains. All are threatened with destruction and desecration by development. A few have already been developed. Where we are now is threatened by the possible extension of the 241 Toll Road,

1. Clappers are a hand-held percussion instrument made from a split elderberry branch. They are a traditional percussion instrument of Juaneño women.

which is planned to be built through the campground, through protected environmental spaces, close to the famous Trestles surf beach, and right over the top of where ancient Juaneño-Acjachema human remains have been reburied. Jimi Castillo points out that there are volunteer helpers on the walk today, and that they are dressed in red T-shirts, should anyone have questions or problems.

We walk through the campground, slowly, led by singers, clappers and rattles. Everyone is singing traditional American Indian songs from the southern California region. Most are one or two lines, sung repetitively. As we walk through the campgrounds on the asphalt road, curious campers come out to see what is going on. A woman tries to take a picture. One of the helpers for the day, a woman in a red T-shirt, darts past me to jump in front of the photo-taker. She tells her not to take a picture. No photos of sacred acts allowed.

We walk about a half mile down the road in the campground to where it ends in a steel bar gate, painted a sunny yellow. The village site is beyond, but on land used by the Marine Base Camp Pendleton, so no one is allowed there. On the other side of the gate is thick brush at least seven feet high, a much more imposing deterrent than the waist-high gate. We circle up. Some people from the campground, adults and children, have joined us. A number of ladies, who are Tuschmal singers, the Juaneño women's singing group, lead a song. Others follow with songs, some singing individually, some asking the group to join.

FIGURE 1.1 *Panhe, a historical village site for the Juaneño–Acjachema. This site was at one point threatened by the proposed extension of the 241 Toll Road.*

FIGURE 1.2 *Panhe is located partly in San Mateo Campgrounds and partly in the Camp Pendleton Marine Base. The Ancestors Walk takes us to this gate that marks the boundary between the two.*

When we walk back, the children are asked to be up front, along with the elders and the Robles family. The late Lillian Robles was one of the founders of this yearly walk, and her children have taken on the fight to preserve sacred sites. Upon reaching the parking lot where we started, we circle up and sing again. The circle breaks and people stay a little while, visiting. Jimi Castillo lets everyone know there are snacks and drinks in the back of his truck. There is also a sign-in sheet to keep track of how many people are here. Then people climb into their vehicles and are off to the next site. We were supposed to be at Putiidhem at 8:30; it is already well past that.

Putiidhem. San Juan Capistrano, at the intersection of Junipera Serra and Camino Capistrano streets. While the previous site was a campground surrounded by wilderness, this is in town. Down the street about four blocks is the Mission San Juan Capistrano. In one direction, the freeway overpass looms. Opposite that, high green hillsides remind us of what this land once must have looked like.

Seventy people are gathered here. They form a large circle on the edge of the site. A chain link fence put up by the company seeking to develop Putiidhem surrounds the site itself.[2] We are all standing on the twenty-foot edge between the fence and the road. In the circle again, we have prayers, songs, and people talking about what this site means to them.

2. Since the time of this Ancestors Walk (2003), this site has been developed into a sports field and arts center for the JSerra School.

FIGURE 1.3 *JSerra High School is the private school that was built on the Putiidhem site.*

FIGURE 1.4 *The JSerra High School Arts Pavilion. The ancient burial ground and village site this is built on is "protected" by capping with eight feet of fill dirt.*

Putiidhem is the location of the "mother village" of the Juaneño. Father Geronimo Boscana, who was at the Mission San Juan Capistrano in the mid-1800s, collected the origin stories of the Juaneño people. According to his writings, they migrated here from the north and the site now called Putiidhem is where they first settled (Harrington 1934). This is also another site where human remains have been found, and reburied.

Now, a small part of the village site, which has remained relatively undeveloped (it has been a farm field, rodeo grounds, and fairgrounds), may be developed into sports fields for a private Catholic high school. The Juaneño Band of Mission Indians, along with groups such as California Cultural Resources Preservation Alliance and the Spirit of Capistrano, is actively fighting to block this development, both through litigation and through public protest. California Cultural Resources Preservation Alliance (CCRPA) is a group of academic and professional anthropologists and archeologists, Juaneño-Acjachema, Gabrieleño-Tongva, and Luiseño peoples, working to preserve archeological and cultural sites in southern California. The Spirit of Capistrano was organized specifically to fight against the development of Putiidhem, and is made up of both Juaneño-Acjachema and non-Indians.

Some Juaneño people I spoke with do favor a plan that would have Putiidhem developed into a playing field, with a cap of a few feet of soil over the existing ground, as is now planned by the private school developers. They argue that this is preferable to the site's being developed into a strip mall or office building. These are difficult issues in Orange County, California, where real estate values are high, and a piece a land being left undeveloped is highly unlikely.

While people are circled up to talk about the site, pray or sing, a bird comes and lands on a man's hat, then moves to the ground at the center of the prayer circle. It stays the whole time we are in the circle.[3] At the end of the circle we come together into a group, people standing close, all touching one another. We sing and repeat a single lined song. It was a very powerful moment.[4] Following the singing and prayer, we stayed and tied strips of red, black, and yellow cloth to the fence that surrounds the site. It was said that each cloth strip represents a prayer.

Newport Back Bay. We park in a parking lot behind a bank off Jamboree Road, in Newport Beach, almost directly across from a high-end housing development on the Back Bay. This development occurred on what the Juaneño-Acjachema consider a sacred site, where

---

3. This incident with the bird has been brought up several times in years since as a special blessing, or as an indication of the special spiritual nature of either the man whose hat was landed on, or the Juaneño people as a whole. I have noticed that any sort of unusual behavior by birds and animals is often remarked upon by American Indian people. I believe this is due to the construction of American Indian identity as both more spiritual than whites, and as more attuned to nature than whites. These themes are further explored in chapter 3.

4. A moment which, for an anthropologist, brings to mind the idea of communitas (Turner 1969).

Juaneño ancestral remains were found. As people arrive, we circle up to pray. We then walk across Jamboree Road, which is a busy six-lane street, at the traffic light, Juaneño-Acjachema elders and the Robles family lead. They asked that the children be up front again, so my daughter and I are close behind the lead, although walking along the sidewalk we string out. We go up the sidewalk on the other side, cars honk as we go by, most likely because one of the elders is carrying an American Flag.[5] Cars, and then some people cycling, stop to ask what we are doing, and a red-shirted helper stops to explain. We walk down to an asphalt drive that leads down to the bay. Jimi Castillo crosses over the chain blocking the drive, which narrows to a dirt path leading to the edge of the wetland. He asks some of the children, some of whom he has given prayer bags, if they would go down the path with him. My daughter was among those who went. They were out of my sight, so I asked her to describe what happened. Cassandra: "We all went, and some kids got prayer bags, and they tied them to bushes in hopes that they would send the prayers to the site."

While the children are down in the ravine, someone else leads us all in a song. When they came back up, we walk back. On the way back there is less singing, people are quiet. This time we circle round the guardhouse at the entrance to the housing development. As we approach, one of the people in the group says to me, "Some guy comes out every year and apologizes, says he didn't know when he bought his house here that it was on a burial ground."

We walk back to the bank parking lot, circle up, and sing again. Again we gather into a close group to sing. After the circle breaks up people hang out and visit awhile. In a picnic area behind the bank there is acorn bread and juice provided by a woman named Joan Kitchen, who is a plant expert and is often at Juaneño events.

Bolsa Chica. We have driven toward the coast. We meet at a protected wetland site, gather in the nature center parking lot. We will walk from here to the site that is threatened. While the city is close here, as in most parts of southern California, when we get out of our cars, we have a view of miles of flat wetlands to one side, and over across Pacific Coast Highway—the ocean.

---

5. At this same point in the Walk in 2002, shortly after the events of 9-11-2001, almost every car that went by honked, and some people shouted things like "yeah America." It was apparent they had no idea what the people were walking for—they were just reacting to the American flag.

As people gather, there is a table with snacks, trail mix, and granola bars. Many people are visiting, waiting while more arrive. Things are running very "late" according to the schedule on the flyer for the walk. No one seems bothered by this; it is expected. We assemble in a circle, Jimi Castillo again opening. While he talked, another man went around the circle, smudging everyone with sage. The burning bundle of sage is held in front of each person. Some people just let the smoke drift over them, some sweep it up over their head and turn in a circle so their whole body is exposed to it. Some pray quietly while they do this.

Jimi Castillo tells us that there are 101 people gathered here. He talks about how this was where, seven years ago, Lillian Robles first decided to gather some people together to walk, to protest the possible destruction of the site. Lillian Robles, now deceased, is a Juaneño-Acjachema woman who was a leader in her community and worked to preserve culturally and archeologically important sites. She is probably best known for involvement in the fight to preserve Pavungna, an important cultural and archeological site on the California State University, Long Beach, campus. Jimi shares that the first year they held this Ancestors Walk, it was just a few people, but Lillian and others helped to save this Bolsa Chica site from being developed. The Ancestors Walk has been held every year since and has grown.

Once everyone has been smudged, there is a prayer. Then we start out, the Robles family and the spiritual leaders in front still, and again asking the children to be up front with them. At one point we walk on the side of a busy street, walking up the embankment to the guardrail, climbing it, and walking the side of the road that is the bridge over the estuary. Once off the road again, we are walking on a dirt path that winds along the side of an inlet. There are dried marsh grasses, and specific plants are marked with flags. These, we had been told earlier, are native plant species that had been planted recently. Seeming symbolic of what has happened to the Juaneño-Acjachema themselves, foreign plant species have encroached upon the land and crowded out the native species. The water of the inlet is at low tide, and on one bank, marking the depth of high tide, is a wide band of trash. Although one is told again and again that everything that goes into storm drains ends up in the sea, it is striking to see the actual trash on the banks of what is supposed to be a protected wetland. Up front they are singing. Further back, where I am, we are mostly quiet.

Prior to starting out, we were told it was a half-mile walk. We walk what seems a long way down the side of the inlet, to a place where some palm trees stand. This place is still called the "log area," even though the large stack of logs that was once here has long since been removed. We stop here, and the path has widened to a dirt road. We circle up. Some people pray and talk. Rebecca Robles, one of Lillian Robles' daughters, says:

> We're all like cups and saucers; we all have a little piece of our tradition, our culture. I might have a part of the handle and I get together with Fran and she might have part of the saucer, and this other person might have part of the cup. When we all get together, we're whole.

Jimi Castillo points out a sign, near where there is a chain-link fence, and says, "Grandma Lillian and I used to love having our picture taken under that sign, it says 'Private Property. No Trespassing.'"

There is more singing. Rebecca Robles comments that some singers have their contemporary songs, and others have their traditional songs. A man says he will sing the Willow Song, differently than the Tuschmal singers do. He says that up and down the coast different people do these songs all a bit differently. The implication is clear: criticisms that people volley about, that this person or that person isn't doing the songs "right" and therefore is not "legitimately Indian" are not valid. The feeling of this whole event is of community building, with comments like this man's and Rebecca's specifically directed at critiquing those who would be divisive.

Pavungna. This site is a part of the campus of California State University, Long Beach. It is a part of campus that has not been developed, and is a shallow valley rolling down from the parking lot. There are old sycamore and oak trees, their height and girth dominating the space.

It is a big space, maybe six acres. There are groupings of trees, and marsh grasses in the far back. People have clearly been here some time, setting up for the event. Toward the right as I walk up, there are three to four large trees around a circular dirt area with a stone fire ring in the center: the dance area. To the left of this dance area, on the edge of it, are loudspeakers, a slightly raised platform with microphones at the front of it. A man is playing a wooden flute. A few people have set up chairs on the edge of the dance area. To the left as one walks down from the parking lot, are tables with food, covered just now, and more empty space to be filled with more food later.

Many more people are gathering; people who went on the walk are now arriving, others came just for this event. More than 200 people are now here. As it is just starting to get dark, an announcement is made that people should come and eat. As at all American Indian events I have attended, elders eat first. We eat, visit. At full dark the fire is set in the center of the dance area. Soon the Bear Dance will begin.

Bear Dance. "You called them down, now you have to deal with them." These are the words of Jimi Castillo, announcing the beginning of the Bear Dance, following his enlisting the voice of the crowd of 200 plus people to "call down the bears from the mountains." Of course, they didn't come from the mountains, but from just up the hill in the parking lot. And of course, they aren't bears... but in the dark, with just the fire for light, the men wearing the bearskins, bent over, moving with a slogging rhythm to the

FIGURE 1.7 *The final destination of Ancestors Walk is the Pavungna village site on the campus of California State University at Long Beach.*

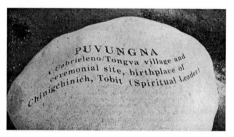

FIGURE 1.8 *The Pavungna site is a historical village for the Gabrieleño-Tongva people as well as the Juaneño-Acjachema.*

FIGURE 1.9 *This prayer stick at Pavungna commemorates the life of Lillian Robles, who worked tirelessly for the preservation of sacred sites.*

drums and imitating the vocalizations of a bear, one is almost tricked to see the bear. Six men in bearskins dance around the fire, while all of us watch. Mostly the dance is an imitation of the movements of a bear, the men bent over, moving slowly. Some of the men vomit. The dance is a healing and spiritual ceremony, Jimi Castillo explains. The vomiting is because they have taken in bad energy, and are vomiting it up.[6] After a while, the announcer says that people may come and "link up" with the bear dancers, to get the medicine they have. People line up to go into the ring, and are smudged with sage before they go in.

Almost everyone wants to dance with the bears, and the entire dance area gets filled with people linked up, touching each other. The bear dancers link up at the end of the line of people, forming what looks like a long "conga line" that spirals around the fire. The drum starts and they all dance around and around the dance ring.

When the Bear Dance ends, all those present depart to go back to their lives in urban and suburban Southern California. Most of the American Indians present at this event do not live on any sort of reservation, but live side-by-side in neighborhoods with Hispanics, Asians, Persians and whites as well as other ethnic and racial groups in multicultural southern California. What then, makes the Juaneño-Acjachema people American Indian? Aren't Indians supposed to live on reservations, have different clothes, and wear their hair long and in braids?

So who, then, are the Juaneño-Acjachema?

The Juaneño-Acjachema are the people who are indigenous to Southern California, mostly in the area now called Orange County. Orange County, known for Disneyland and sprawling suburbia, was once scrubsage chaparral, old-growth California live oak and scrub oak forests. It was home to a fairly peaceful people who took what they needed directly from the land and sea with little interference with the natural ecosystems. Then it became a place, under Spanish control, of Missions, ranches of cattle and sheep, and crops grown mostly to supply the Spanish army (Jackson and Castillo 1995). Later, under United States control, it became an agricultural center, known for fruit and nut trees: almonds, avocado and, of course, oranges. The Juaneño-Acjachema people have

---

6. This is found in several other cultures also, where a healer, through some ritual process, takes in bad energy or sickness, and then expels it from his or her body through vomiting.

been here all along. They were the labor that built the Missions; they worked the ranches, working cattle and training horses; they picked the almonds and fruit. Often, in a racist community, it was expedient to de-emphasize, or even conceal, one's identity as American Indian.

Like many California tribes, their first contacts were with the Span-ish. Once the U.S. took over the area, they were already in the background. Since their land was already overtaken, there was no need for the U.S. gov-ernment to make treaties with them. Minimal efforts made in the mid-1800s to formalize relations with California tribes neglected to include the Juaneño-Acjachema, as it did many other California tribes. So they remained unacknowledged by the U.S. government, without a reservation, and with a sprawling suburbia emerging in their homeland.

The Juaneño-Acjachema do not have Federal Acknowledgement of their status as an American Indian tribe. Such Acknowledgement would gain them certain financial benefits, but more to the point, it is taken as a legitimation of their American Indian-ness in U.S. society. The com-plexities of Federal Acknowledgement will be discussed in chapter 3.

Questions of identity, of "having a culture" and of existing as a social and political entity come to be crucial not only for individuals struggling with identity issues, but for a community seeking Federal Acknowledgement and the concurrent rights that go with it. For many Juaneño-Acjachema that I spoke to and interviewed, acknowledge-ment of their Juaneño-Acjachema identity entails their right to pro-tect their past and preserve a future for their community.

The Community

Although they consider San Juan Capistrano as the origination point of their community, Juaneño-Acjachema people live all over Orange County, Los Angeles County, Riverside County, and San Diego County. Also, as with other people in this highly mobile world we live in, Juaneño-Acjachema people have migrated all over the United States. San Juan Capistrano remains a community center politically and emotionally, if not demographically.

The Juaneño Band of Mission Indians, Acjachema Nation,[7] has its tribal office in San Juan Capistrano, which is also where the Mission is.

---

7. www.juaneno.com/ shorthanded JBMI in this book, designated Petition 84A in Bureau of Acknowledgement and Research (BAR) publications, and shorthanded JBA in their texts.

Mission San Juan Capistrano cultural events also tend to be Juaneño-Acjachema community events. Swallows Day, the Swallows Day Parade, and Mission Days at the Mission are times for the Juaneño people to put on traditional regalia, put together displays of basketry or beadwork, have booths selling fry bread or other food, and have skits and programs displaying Juaneño-Acjachema culture, history and song. The issue of what is "really traditional Juaneño" aside;[8] these events are a time for the Juaneño-Acjachema community to get together, "be Juaneño," and be public about being Juaneño. This can include those who are in conflict about who is "the tribe." At one of these events, I was at the display table with the basket-weaving ladies from the Juaneño Band of Mission Indians, Acjachema Nation (JBMI). There were mutterings—"oh look at *him* show up! What is *he* doing here!" It was the leader of another political faction of the tribe, standing along the side walkway in the Mission, alongside some older women. This is a "rival" group, and "rival" leader both in terms of contesting for who is legitimately Juaneño, who is the legitimate leader of the Juaneño, and who had the right to petition for federal recognition of the tribe.[9] This man and the women he was with were probably saying among themselves things very similar to the things the ladies around me were saying.

The Research Project

My contacts with the Juaneño-Acjachema community began in 1997 through work on the American Indian Health Project, being conducted at that time by Laura Williams, M.D., M.P.H., out of the Center for Health Policy Research at the University of California at Irvine. Working as a graduate student research assistant on this project, I was introduced to the American Indian community in Southern California generally and the Juaneño-Acjachema community specifically. Most of the specific data collection for this book took place 2000-2003.

The people who were interviewed, given questionnaires, and who participated in events where I conducted participant observer research,

---

8. The Acjachema people did not make fry bread; a traditional food would be the acorn mush they ate as a staple, but it is unlikely it would be profitable to sell—I am told it is, at best, bland.

9. This individual is designated an "interested party" in the BAR Federal Acknowledgement Petition publications. Another faction of the Juaneño-Acjachema, calling itself the Juaneño Band of Mission Indians, is designated Petition 84B by the BAR, and referred to as JBB in their publications.

were all people who self-identified as Juaneño-Acjachema. Although I had some contact with and collected some data with other groups, the vast majority of data collection took place with a group calling themselves The Juaneño Band of Mission Indians, Acjachema Nation (JBMI). Some research was done with people in a second faction of the tribe, at that time led by Sonia Johnston, who personally facilitated my research with women in her tribe. No formal contacts were made with the leader of the third faction, David Belardes, although some individuals who were at various times associated with his group did talk to me and contribute to this project. There was a great deal of suspicion and animosity toward this third faction and its leader among people I was working with in the other two factions. Several people made it very clear early on that if I spoke to Belardes, they would have nothing more to do with me. The prudent move seemed to be to leave out any attempt to contact that group formally. How much that may have affected the data for this project is unknown. However, people in all three groups know each other, some families are split across the groups, and people move between the groups. One of the first women I interviewed had been in Belardes's group at the beginning of the study, was then in Sonia Johnston's group, and as far as I know is now in the JBMI. I have serious doubts that there is significant cultural difference across the three groups.

A major focus of the research project was the pregnancy beliefs and practices of Juaneño-Acjachema women. Research on this took place in the context of learning about the community generally, and the behaviors of people striving to be American Indian, and specifically Juaneño; in a social setting that is, at times, hostile to their holding that identity.

Data was collected in a number of phases. Ethnographic data collection through participant observation at community events (formal and informal) went on throughout this process. Preliminary informal focus groups and individual freelisting questionnaires as well as casual discussion of the project topics were conducted. Freelisting is a data collection technique in which an individual is asked a question about a semantic domain, and the response is a list of items in that domain. Juaneño women were asked a set of questions, like "What should a woman do to keep her baby healthy while pregnant?" and "What might be dangerous to a woman and her baby while she is pregnant?" These questions elicited lists that were used as preliminary data, and to contribute to the creation of a questionnaire on risks and practices during pregnancy.

In-depth interviews with ten women about their pregnancy and birth experiences were conducted. These were tape-recorded, transcribed, and analyzed. Finally, a questionnaire was created reflecting statements women had made in the preliminary work and early interviews. This questionnaire was administered at social community events, including, with the approval and help of the Tribal Council of the Juaneño Band of Mission Indians, Acjachema Nation, an event following one of their General Council Meetings. This was especially helpful, as the General Council Meetings brought in a large number of people, many of whom would travel long distances to come, and thus would not have been easily accessed for data collection.

The questionnaire data were analyzed and written up elsewhere (Coffman 2004). This book focuses on the ethnographic and interview data. Issues of individual and community identity, and the reproduction of that community and identity through mother-daughter transmission of cultural knowledge during pregnancy is a general theme of the book.

The Scope of this Book

This book is not intended to be the final word on the Juaneño-Acjachema. Nor is this book intended to argue for or against Federal Acknowledgement or in any way contribute to that determination. The research conducted for this book is limited to the observations of the author, and the interviews and the questionnaires conducted by the author. The author, it should be noted, is an outsider to both the Southern California and the Juaneño community. This type of research is traditional in anthropology: the anthropologist (usually white) goes to some foreign place and studies some foreign people (usually nonwhite). The colonial underpinnings are apparent. Historically in anthropology, there has been the claim of objectivity in this distance, in this study of "the other." Most anthropologists today, including myself, acknowledge that true objectivity is impossible. There is some subjectivity in an individual's understanding of what they are seeing, their interpretation of what is being said to them. The goal is to tell some kind of a truth, while acknowledging one's position. This book exemplifies such an attempt at truth.

Who is Juaneño-Acjachema?

This question is the topic of debate, discussion, political factioning, and even threats among the Juaneño-Acjachema people. In 2007, following the Proposed Finding Against Federal Acknowledgement, the JBMI modified their membership rolls in accordance with the genealogical findings of the BIA. It was necessary to do this to have any hope of gaining federal recognition. However, a large number of people who had been members, and who identified strongly as Acjachema, some of whom had worked diligently for federal recognition, were now suddenly not Juaneño. There is a great deal of anger about this. For example, as I stood on the sidewalk taking pictures of the Swallows Day Parade in the Spring of 2010, I overheard comments of some people behind me who were apparently former members of the JBMI who had been dis-enrolled. As the JBMI parade group went by, they had a series of comments, which were overwhelmingly negative, about the group and the current tribal chair specifically.

As the majority of the research for this book was being conducted, this hadn't happened yet, but there were discussions and debates even then over who was and who was not Juaneño. As an anthropologist studying ethnic identity, I took individuals' identification of themselves as Juaneño at face value. I am neither a genealogist, nor a historian. More importantly, I, as an outsider, have no right to determine who is and who is not a member of this or any other particular ethnic group.

Overview of the Book

Chapter 2 of the book is an overview of the history and traditional culture of the Juaneño-Acjachema in Southern California. The next chapter looks at the community today. This includes a look at the federal recognition process, as well as how individuals enact their Juaneño-Acjachemem Indian identity in their daily lives. Chapter 4 examines the reproduction data, looking at the pregnancy experiences of the several women I interviewed in-depth. These serve to highlight differences in practice between the Juaneño and non-Indians in some key areas of pregnancy risk and post-partum practice. They also highlight the importance of the mother-daughter relationship in teaching women to be not just mothers, but Juaneño-Acjachema mothers. It is not just that biological human beings are made via "human reproduction," it is that *persons*, with a culture and a society that they are part of, are made. The final chapter discusses the outcome of the Federal Acknowledgement petition process and community reaction to it.

chapter 2

Juaneño-Acjachema History and Culture

In 1540, American Indians had their first documented contact with Europeans; at this time there were approximately 310,000 Indians in California (Thorton 1987). In 1769, Spanish colonization began with the establishment of the Mission at San Diego, and by 1863 approximately 80,000 Indians were forced to labor in 23 missions from San Diego in the south to Sonoma in the north (Guest 1983).

Spain moved north into the area in order to create a geographic and political buffer to protect silver mines further south from foreign attack (Jackson and Castillo 1995). The process of developing an area in which they had control required the development of a colony, this included control over the local population. This control was gained through the Mission system (Jackson and Castillo 1995). The Missions provided a way to physically control and acculturate the indigenous people to become productive workers, and to create areas where there could be Spanish settlement, thus solidifying Spain's political control.

Following baptism, Indians were confined to the Mission where they were expected to labor to build and then to support the Mission (Jackson and Castillo 1995, Fogel 1988, Guest 1983, Costo 1987, Dias 1996). Unmarried women were confined to barracks. Health conditions were poor, and their diet was much less adequate compared to their diet prior to their being taken into the Mission. Contagious disease such as measles, smallpox, and influenza decimated the Indians living in the Missions. Unmarried women who were confined to the barracks were severely punished by the priests for abortion or infanticide, even though these pregnancies were very often due to rape by Spanish soldiers. Individuals who ran away or resisted were hunted down and captured, and people were often beaten, incarcerated, or maimed to quell resistance. Many have argued that this was a period in which the Acjachema people were enslaved and abused by the Catholic Mission system.

On Oct. 30, 1775, Fr. Lasuen, Lieutenant Ortega, and a small group of Spanish soldiers arrived at what is now San Juan Capistrano to begin a Mission there (Engelhardt 1922). According to the Catholic historian Engelhardt (1922), the Acjachema people were welcoming; they helped to start on the buildings. However, shortly after the arrival of the Spanish, there was an uprising at the San Diego Mission. They buried two large bells that had been brought along for the new church, and returned to San Diego to aid in quelling the uprising (Engelhardt 1922). It was a full year before the Spanish returned. Father Junipero Serra, two other priests, and an escort of eleven soldiers arrived at the site where Lasuen had previously erected a large wooden cross on October 31, and held the first High Mass at the site on November 1 (Engelhardt 1922).

Thus, the Mission in San Juan Capistrano was founded Nov. 1, 1776 by Father Junipera Serra, at a place called *sajivit* or *Quanis-savit* by the Acjachema people (Harrington 1934, see also O'Neil and Evans 1980).The Spanish called all the peoples of the Americas "Indians" continuing the misnomer begun by Columbus some 200 years prior. These specific people, Junipero Serra called "Juaneño" or "Juan's children." This reflected the general attitude of the Franciscan missionaries toward indigenous peoples they encountered: they were like children, unable to care for themselves, and needed the care and supervision of the priests. However, as will be seen in this chapter, the people Father Serra encountered had a well-developed society, and had provided for themselves in this place for many centuries before the coming of the Spanish.

It was not long before conflict arose; namely, abuse of the indigenous peoples by the Spanish:

[T]wo pagan [sic] chiefs had come to join the Mission. . .one chief had complained to Fr. Serra that the soldier Manual Robles had assaulted his wife, wherefore the Fr. Presidente demanded the removal of the soldier… Recruited from the scum of society in Mexico, frequently convicts and jailbirds, it is not surprising that the mission guards…should be guilty of such and similar crimes at nearly all the Missions. It does amaze, however, that such a scandal could happen within three weeks of the founding of the Mission. (Engelhardt 1922:8)

At contact, there was an estimated population of 15,200 indigenous people in the region surrounding the five southern missions—Los Angeles to Baja (Cook 1971). The Juaneño-Acjachema population in 1769 was approximately 4,000 (Dias 1996). The number of people who lived within the confines of the Mission was a relatively small proportion of this. In 1783, there were 383 converts living in the Mission; 544 in 1783; 741 in 1790 (Engelhardt 1922). The Juaneño territory was approximately 1,500 square miles between Aliso Creek in the northwest and Aqua Hacienda Creek in the south, inland to Santiago Peak, southeast to the east of Palomar Mountain, and to the southern slope of San Jose Mountain (Dias 1996).

map of geographic area

Culture and Society

Most of what we know about the Acjachema comes from the writings of a Franciscan priest, Father Geronimo Boscana. Boscana was the Superior priest in San Juan Capistrano Mission 1812-1826 (Harrington 1934). The priests of all the California Missions were given a questionnaire to report to their superiors on the peoples they were working with. Boscana returned his survey, but then he continued to write about the Acjachema people, their culture, and their social practices. The work was found among his things following his death; it is unclear whether he intended it for publication (Harrington 1934). It was published first in 1846 by Alfred Robinson, and later translated again and extensively annotated by the anthropologist John P. Harrington (1934). Harrington also did extensive ethnographic work with the Juaneño in the 1930s. He made voice recordings of the Juaneño language, collected stories and songs, and other ethnographic data. His extensive field notes remain largely unpublished. The vast collection is held by the Smithsonian and can be accessed for further research through that institution. Boscana's writings, as translated by Harrington, remains the primary source for information on the Juaneño-Acjachema.

Juaneño-Acjachema Traditional Culture and Society

Subsistence Practices

The pre-contact Acjachema were subsistence foragers whose dietary staple was acorns, gathered by the women from the old growth oak trees that grew along watersheds, creeks, and in the foothills and local mountains (Kroeber 1971b, Harrington 1934). Although they did not have domesticated plants and animals, the Acjachema managed the growth of plants needed for food and basket materials through controlled burns (Cook 1941).

Acorns, as a food resource, required extensive processing to remove the poisonous tannic acid. This was accomplished by grinding acorns into a flour and then leaching them in a basket or a sand basin (Gifford 1971). Large boulders with holes that were used for acorn grinding can still be found in southern California, often near streams.

Other food sources made use of the extensive wildlife and rich ecology of the local area. Men hunted a wide variety of game. Other grains such as chia and buckeye were also collected and ground for consumption.

FIGURE 2.1 *White sage, used ceremonially by Juaneño-Acjachema.*

Settlements shifted seasonally, taking advantage of the ripening of acorns in the foothill and mountain California live oak forests in the fall, and the milder weather of the coast in the winter. In the coastal settlements, a major staple food was shellfish. Similar subsistence patterns were found among most California coastal groups, with few having any form of cultivation (Kroeber 1971a). Anthropologist Alfred Kroeber (1971b) points out that the wide variety of food sources in the area was a buffer against shortages of any one type of food. No reported famines appear in either oral or documented history of the region pre-colonially (Kroeber 1971b).

Political System

Kroeber claims that for California Indians generally, the term "tribe" as denoting a group organized as a political whole does not apply, but rather that the term would denote an ethnic group (1971). Political organization in all of California tended to be of smaller groups of kin and close associates, often with attachment to a particular locale, "a few miles of stream or valley" (Kroeber 1971: 27).

Boscana reported the Juaneño-Acjachema had a complex political structure, consisting of a chiefdom and a class structure (Harrington 1934). The chief was called a *Noot, noonutum* (pl) (Harrington 1934:107). There was also a general council, called a *Publem*. The chief had named officers: speakers, messengers, and a director of rituals. Chieftainship was inherited, passed from father to son. The Noot and Publem had privileges others did not, such as entering the sacred space where the Chinigchinich (god) figure was. They were given deference in social interaction and wore clothing specific to their office as Noot and Publem.

There is a lack of clarity in Boscana's writing regarding female leaders. He notes that if a chief has no son, then the title will pass to his daughter, but that the actual ruling will be done by her nearest male relative, and the title passed on to her son as soon as he is born.

> In the succession of these chieftainships, women also entered, when males were lacking. She could marry whoever she pleased…but the husband… was never recognized [as chief]…nor did he have command, but they only recognized the woman. But she did not govern, or perform the functions of chief, but the government was exercised by another, an uncle or a grandfather, the nearest of blood. But the first male whom she bore, immediately was declared chief. (Harrington 1934: 31-32)

Kroeber (1971), Harrington (1934) and Boscana are all adamant that women were never chiefs. However, Boscana, in relating the tale of the origins of the Acjachema people told to him by the Acjachema themselves, states that a woman named Coronne came down from the northern site *Sejat* with her father, who was the chief, and with a contingency of people wishing to relocate. The chief goes back to Sejat, leaving his daughter as chief. There is no part of this that mentions Coronne not really leading them, or some other male relative that is the actual decision-maker. I suggest that it is possible that both Boscana, and later Kroeber, living in relatively patriarchal societies themselves, were unable to accept the possibility that there were, in fact, women chiefs among the Acjachema.[1]

---

1. The author wishes to acknowledge her own potential bias in this assessment: Being a female in a relatively non-patriarchal society, I am inclined to see the possibility of women as leaders.

Settlements contained 100-200 people and were subdivided into clan or lineage segments of hamlet size (25-35 people) (Harrington 1934, Kroeber 1971, 1976). Each village was a ritually integrated political group, an autonomous "tribelet" with its own chief (Harrington 1934). There were property rights over production capital, territoriality, inter-group warfare, ceremonial based supra-family exchange networks, and valuables (i.e. shell money and trade beads) (Dias 1996, Jackson and Castillo 1995). However, even with the Noot and Publem, the social structure was still primarily based on kin groups.

Kinship

Among the Juaneño-Acjachema specifically, there were clans and lineages, with descent traced primarily through males and alliances formed through marriage (Harrington 1934, Dias 1996). Boscana includes accounts of marriage initiating in several ways: a man courting a particular woman, then asking her parents for her in marriage; a man simply approaching parents and not the girl; children who were "wed" (betrothed) during early childhood; and a Noot or son of a Noot from another village demanding a girl from her parents under threat of violence. Boscana also notes that divorce is allowed.

Boscana has a description of bride service for the Juaneño (Harrington 1934). A man was to come to his wife's home, and lives with her and her family for fifteen days and hunts for them. There was also an expectation that the woman take on all of the household chores of food preparation and care of the household, so that, as Boscana put it, he could see if she was a hard worker and capable in these household tasks. During this time they were not in a conjugal union, as they were not officially married yet. Just prior to the marriage, a man may give the bride's parents small gifts of valuables.

Religious Practices

Shamanism, in which a religious practitioner enters a trance state and interacts directly with the spirit realm, existed throughout the California culture area (Bean 1992, Kroeber 1971a). The primary function of the shaman was to cure disease. There was diagnosis by singing, dancing, smoking tobacco, sometimes trance; a foreign or hostile object in the body was often the cause of illness. This object was removed by sucking. There might also be manipulation of the body, brushing of body, and the blowing of tobacco smoke or spit, to facilitate extraction of the object. Among the Acjachema, shaman were called *Pul, Puula,* pū uplum (pl.) (Harrington 1934). The pūuplum also functioned as village elders, whose rank was as high as a chief.

Kroeber (1971a, 1976) noted that in southern California shaman-istic power can be used for good or evil; disease as well as healing is believed to be caused by shamans. Thus, shamans unsuccessful in heal-ing a person might be blamed for the death. He might even be killed in retribution for it, or simply out of fear that he might harm others in the village. These kinds of deaths were blamed on other communities, and might spark intertribal warfare.

In California there were several kinds of "specialist" shamans (Kroeber 1971a, 1976). There was a "rain doctor," who could bring rain. There was a "bear doctor" or bear shaman who had the power to turn himself into a grizzly bear (Kroeber 1971a). These "bear doctors" still exist today in the form of the Bear Dance described at the beginning of this book.

CHINIGCHINICH RELIGION

The Chinigchinich[2] religion was found in the southern California region, including the Juaneño, and the Gabrieleño-Tongva, the Acjachema's neighbors to the north (roughly the Los Angeles county area). Accord-ing to the creation story recorded by Father Boscana, Chinigchinich was a god-like being who presented himself following the death of Oüiot[3] (Harrington 1934). Oüiot was the chief of the first beings to inhabit the earth. These beings were not humans, and there is no clear description of them that was given to Boscana. These creatures subsisted by con-suming soil. As related in the tale told to Fr. Boscana, Chinigchinich ap-pears, offers to get them something else to eat, and proceeds to change them into spirit-animals, and then creates humans. Chinigchinich then sets up all the rules for living that people must follow, with punishment of disease and death if one does not follow the rules (Harrington 1934).

Rites of the Chinigchinich religion centered on a ceremonial struc-ture. This was a brush enclosure, with no roof, called a *wankech* (Kroe-ber 1976). Specific ceremonial items were kept there, including a coyote pelt filled with objects like feathers, horns, claws, and birds' beaks. In

---

2. Also appears spelled Chinigchinix.
3. Wiyot in Kroeber 1976.

particular, parts of the condor were kept in the pelt, along with some arrowheads. The enclosure also contained a sand painting. The *wankech* was sacred space, voices were kept low, and the uninitiated were not allowed to enter (Kroeber 1976, Harrington 1934).

JIMSONWEED (TOLUÁCHE) CULT

Another religious practice was the Jimsonweed cult. Kroeber (1976) claims that the Jimsonweed cult was passed from the Luiseño to the Juaneño and then on to the Gabrieleño.

As related to Boscana by Acjachema people who were at the Mission San Juan Capistrano in the mid-1800s, boys at age of six were given either a tobacco drink (*Pibat*, Harrington 1934; *Pivat* in Kroeber 1976) or a drink made from *Toluáche*. *Toluáche*, common name Jimsonweed, is *Datura stramonium*, a plant with hallucinogenic properties. However, in larger amounts it can also cause vomiting, diarrhea, convulsions, and death (Heller 2009). When under the influence of one of these drinks, the boys then fast for three or four days, and do not sleep. They experience visions during this time in which they see and communicate with an animal spirit. This animal spirit is then the boy's guardian spirit (Harrington 1934). Animals seen were often a bear, coyote, raven, or rattlesnake.

After boys completed the ordeal and had the vision, they were scarred: plant material, ground into a powder, was put on the skin of their arm or thigh in a design and then lit. The wound is left untreated so that it scars (Harrington 1934).

Puberty Rites

At puberty boys underwent another rite of initiation, which involved further ordeals. These included being whipped with stinging nettles or having ants put on them. The purpose was said to increase endurance and strength (Harrington 1934, Kroeber 1976). At this time the boys received instruction on how to behave as adults. Certain foods were forbidden for the duration of the initiation: acorns, chia, and certain meats. Some meats were forbidden until they had, as adults, fathered 2-3 children (Harrington 1934).

Girls also had puberty rites. Kroeber notes that for southern California generally, "direct physiological treatment [of the girl] is needed to ensure future health," (Kroeber 1971a: 50). This includes the maintenance of warmth, so the girl must not drink cold water and must bathe only in heated water. In fact, the girl is "roasted."

Boscana describes this procedure (Harrington 1934). Following a girl's menarche, there was a grave-shaped, shallow pit dug. This was filled with rocks and burning coals. When the rocks are heated, the coals are removed. The heated rocks were laid over with California Mugwort branches (called *Pacsil*). The girl lies on the rocks, and is covered. She stays this way and fasts for 2-3 days. The roasting pit is decorated with feathers and shell beads. Older women sing, their faces painted black.[4] Unmarried women dance at intervals around the initiate. This was a feast day for the whole group, with distribution of goods, including shell beads (Harrington 1934). Boscana notes that the first-born daughter of a chief is circumcised. A spiritual leader "made with a flint a little cut in the girl's private parts," (Harrington 1934: 22).

During the ritual, she was instructed on how to be a woman, including admonishments to work hard. Kroeber (1971a) notes similar adolescent rites for women among the Luiseño. He additionally notes the use of a head-scratcher, used so that the young woman does not touch her own head during the ceremony; and the use of the deer-hoof rattle as a percussion instrument during the ceremony.

In northern California, the girl was thought of as ritually dangerous at this time, as were all women while menstruating. Kroeber (1971a) says these beliefs were present in the south but where given less importance than the need for physiological treatment of the girl to ensure her future health.

Van Gennep (1960) wrote that rites of passage, rituals that mark and facilitate the transition from one social status to the next, contain three stages: separation, liminality, and incorporation. For the Acjachema girls in traditional society, there was a clear separation stage in which the girls were brought to special sites where the rituals took place. In forays into the local wilderness areas with Juaneño women from the basket-weaving group, to look for and gather basket-weaving materials, I was brought to several places where there were ancient rock paintings. One of these was a site with large boulders beside a creek. Climbing on top of the boulders, one finds the deep circular holes made

---

4. Boscana apparently was not only told about these ceremonies, but witnessed them, as he complained that he thought the song they sang ugly, and that he never understood what they were saying in it. This strongly suggests that the Acjachema people were carrying on their religious and cultural practices even while at the Mission.

FIGURE 2.2 *Grinding stones, used by pre-colonial Acjachema populations for processing acorns, can be found throughout wilderness areas in Southern California. This one is on display in Mission San Juan Capistrano.*

by Acjachema women grinding their acorns on the boulders. On the creek-side of the boulder were rock-paintings. I was told by the women I was with that this was a site where girls were initiated.

The liminal stage is one in which the initiate is between statuses (Van Gennep 1960). Sometimes, this is likened to death. This similarity is apparent with the Juaneño girl lying in a grave-like pit, covered, as if buried. In most initiation rites, the liminal stage involves some sort of physical trial. For the Acjachema girl, along with lying in her heated hole, she eats and drinks little for three days (Harrington 1934). She must undergo a tobacco-eating ordeal, and undergoes tattooing of her face, breasts, and arms. The tattoos are made by pricking the skin with cactus thorns and rubbing the wounds with charcoal (Harrington 1934). She emerges from her "grave" as a new person with the new status of adult woman, completing the ritual with Van Gennep's third stage of incorporation.

Material Culture

Overall, the material culture of the peoples of the South California area could be characterized as minimalistic. People neither had, nor desired, a great deal of material goods. Most clothing was made of buckskin or plant fibers. Women wore skirts of plant fibers or rabbit skins; men wore either nothing or buckskin folded around the hips. In cool weather a blanket woven of rabbit pelts was used, and sometimes worn as a cape. There were sandals of yucca fiber; and women wore a basketry cap (Kroeber 1971a). This cap was often used to aid in carrying a burden-basket with a strap across the top of one's head. Individuals reproduce this attire for dancing at Pow Wows or representing their tribe at some community events, such as the annual walk in the Swallows Day Parade in San Juan Capistrano. However, they generally wear a skin-colored shirt or leotard, foregoing the traditional upper-body nudity.

Houses were a frame of branches, covered with earth, skins or plant fibers in various forms throughout southern California (Kroeber 1971a). Acjachema houses were generally structured of bent saplings, in a curved dome shape, interwoven with Tule fibers. One community member has such a house, or *kiicha*, reproduced in her front lawn. In years past, this kiicha has been a part of the Swallows Day Parade, appearing on the tribe's float.

Textiles

> "Basketry is unquestioningly the most developed art in California." (Kroeber 1971a:14)

FIGURE 2.3 *Juncus, used for basket weaving. Photo taken at Mission San Juan Capistrano.*

FIGURE 2.4 *Deergrass, another basket-making material. Both juncus and deergrass grow wild in Southern California, but are threatened by the encroachment of invasive species.*

In southern California, they made coiled baskets on a foundation of straws of *Epicampes rigens* (deergrass); sewed with sumac or Juncus (Kroeber 1971a). The Juaneño neither wove cloth nor made pottery (Kroeber 1971a). Their coiled baskets met all of their carrying, storage, and cooking needs. Coiled baskets lined with tar or pinesap were watertight, and used for cooking. As described to me by a Juaneño woman, a liquid—water or acorn porridge, for example—was heated and cooked by the adding of heated stones to the basket. One had to keep stirring the stones, though, because if they sat on the bottom they would burn through the basket.

Juaneño Life After the Spanish Came

The arrival of the Spanish and the founding of Mission San Juan Capistrano marked a turning point in the life of the Acjachema people. The Spanish came, founded their Mission, bringing people into the Mission walls, some willingly, some likely not. These "neophytes" as they were called, lived a regimented life of prayers, meals, and work (Jackson and Castillo 1995, Jackson 1994, Fogel 1988). While families could have their own hut or small adobe house, young unmarried women were kept in locked dorms when not in some supervised task like soap-making or working in the tannery (Jackson and Castillo 1995, Fogel 1988).

FIGURE 2.5 *The Old Stone Church at the Mission, built by the labor of Juaneño–Acjachema people. The church was destroyed December 8, 1812, by an earthquake that killed 42 Juaneño–Acjachema worshippers inside.*

FIGURE 2.6 *The Mission bells courtyard.*

It is sometimes suggested that the Mission system brought an improvement to the lives of the Indians, and that one of these improvements was through better diet. The Indians of Southern California had a diet that was both abundant and varied (Cook 1941, Kroeber 1971b). The fact that the Spanish found a permanent settlement of several hundred people where they chose to build the Mission San Juan Capistrano is a clear indication that the people of the Capistrano Valley were not on the brink of starvation. Moreover, anthropologists have documented that foragers living in much less abundant ecosystems, have not only an adequate diet but worked less than the average person today (Sahlins 1972). Many scholars, moreover, have argued that the diet of the neophytes in the Mission system was inadequate in both calories and protein (Jackson and Castillo 1995, Fogel 1988, Cook 1971a).

The Mission system brought not only a new religion, but a new political economy. This was a political economy built largely on the slave labor of the indigenous people. As has been extensively documented by Jackson and Castillo (1995), the labor of the Juaneño and other indigenous people in what was to become California, built the mission buildings but worked in agriculture and ranching. They raised sheep, cattle, and horses; they planted grain crops, vegetable crops, and grapes for wine. They tanned hides, made soap, and aged wine. These products did not, in the vast majority, go to feeding and clothing the neophytes who were doing the work. The vast majority went to the Spanish army (Jackson and Castillo 1995).

In the Missions, poor nutrition coupled with poor sanitation and overwork contributed to an exceedingly high mortality rate (Dias 1996, Jackson and Castillo 1995). This was exacerbated greatly by the Europeans having brought with them diseases, like measles and influenza, that the Indians had no immunity to. Infants, children, and women of childbearing age were particularly likely to die, leaving the Missions with an abnormal demographic structure, in which there were as many as two men for every woman (Jackson and Castillo 1995).

The Mission system in California spanned the years 1776-1834. In 1833, following the independence of Mexico from Spain in 1821, it was declared that the Missions would be secularized. This meant that the Mission buildings and lands would no longer be the property of the Catholic church. It was declared that the Indians should be freed and that Mission lands and property should be parceled out to them. This plan, which was implemented in 1834, went only partly into effect: the Mission's property was dispersed, but generally not to the Indians.

> [S]ecularization did not bring about an immediate
> change in the status of the converts living in the mis-
> sions; their emancipation was a gradual rather than an

immediate process. Moreover much of the land, buildings, and other property of the missions did not pass
into the hands of the converts. Most of the Indians living in the missions in 1834 mostly used the breakdown
of the Franciscan regime as an opportunity to leave.
(Jackson and Castillo 1995: 90)

In San Juan Capistrano, an "Indian Pueblo" was created in 1833
via a decree by Governor José Figueroa (Jackson and Castillo 1995).
This was a small township of Juaneño on what had been Mission lands,
initially with its own municipal government. The management of the
town was soon taken over by a civil administrator appointed by the provincial government. This led to problems for the Juaneño in the pueblo.

The return of Indians to a form of subjugation
similar to the social control previously exercised by the
Franciscans disrupted the development of the Indian
pueblo. In the late 1830s, the Indians at San Juan Capistrano complained about the administrator, especially
his attempts to get the Indians to work for his personal
benefit. Moreover the Indians complained about the
alienation of mission lands and goods into the hands of
local settlers. (Jackson and Castillo 1995: 92)

These circumstances led to Juaneño leaving the Pueblo and San
Juan Capistrano. According to Jackson and Castillo (1995), in 1834
there were 861 Indians in San Juan Capistrano, by 1840, 500 remained, of whom only 100 lived in the pueblo. The pueblo was dis-
solved in 1841 by the provincial government, its lands distributed to
Indians and local settlers.

Following secularization of the missions and the end of the pueblo,
Juaneño moved into work as ranch-hands, *vaqueros*, and domestic workers. They were free to move around, and did so, mostly in the pursuit of
work (Jackson and Castillo 1995). In 1845 the buildings and remaining
lands of San Juan Capistrano sold at public auction, purchased by John
Forster and James McKinley (Orange County Historical Society 2010).
It became the private home of the Forster family.

California Becomes Part of the United States

Following the Mexican-American war (1848), the Treaty of Guadalupe Hidalgo ceded California to the United States. It also guaranteed Indians in California rights to the land they occupied (Heizer 1974). After the discovery of gold in California, gold miners "descended upon the Sierra Nevada and surrounding Native territories" in large numbers (Hodge 1993:4). Even while the federal government sought to protect the Indians, state laws "enslaved Indians and institutionalized the legal kidnapping of Indian children for labor and sexual exploitation," (Hodge 1993:4; see also Hurtado 1988, Heizer 1974). Passed by the California Legislature in 1850, *An Act for the Government and Protection of Indians* allowed for the removal of California Indians from their land, separated Indian children and adults from their families and broke up families through an indenture system, and allowed for the "hiring out" of "vagrant" American Indians to the highest bidder (Johnson-Dodds 2002). Under this Act, California Indian adults and children were not supposed to be indentured by force. It was up to the Justice of the Peace to both approve the indenture and ascertain that the child was not being indentured against his or her will (Johnson-Dodds 2002). However, numerous accounts exist of California Indian children being brought into indenture forcibly, often through the killing of their parents (Johnson-Dodds 2002, Heizer 1974). The following is an excerpt from a letter from a field officer to his Captain, dated May 31, 1861:

> I have the honor to report that there are several parties of citizens now engaged in stealing or taking by force Indian children from the district in which I have been ordered to operate against the Indians....I am reliably informed that as many as forty or fifty Indian children have been taken through Long Valley within the past few months and sold both in and out of the county. [Heizer 1974:229]

So although the law specifically states that the children being indentured enter such indenture willingly, in practice this was not the case. These indenture and vagrancy laws were not repealed until 1937 (Johnson-Dodds 2002).

During this time period, Indians in California were afforded few legal rights. As set out under the 1850s Acts, Justices of the Peace had full jurisdiction over complaints involving Indians, without the ability of Indians to appeal. Also, a white man could not be convicted based on the testimony of an Indian (Johnson-Dodds 2002).

The Unratified Treaty of Temecula

As the gold rush brought whites to California in vast numbers, conflicts between whites and Indians increased. The U.S. government sought to control the Indians and ease the level of conflict through formalized relations with the California Indians. In 1851-52 eighteen treaties were negotiated by three federal representatives with people from California Indian tribes (Johnson-Dodds 2002, Field 1999). BIA Commissioner O.M. Wozencraft, working under the auspices of the California Land Claims Act, called for all American Indian leaders to meet with him. Wozencraft negotiated with American Indians he contacted at Temecula, and this was as close as he got to the Juaneño. The Juaneño did not send a representative to this meeting, and were not a part of the treaty. It is unclear how this announcement to meet was made and how much effort was made to contact all tribe leaders. The overall process of arranging the treaties was highly questionable. The people who signed the treaties may not have understood what they were signing and were themselves largely illiterate, and it is unlikely that those who signed the treaties represented anything but the smallest local village they lived in (Field 1999, Heizer 1972, Hurdato 1988).

The treaties reserved approximately 11,700 square miles, or 7.5 million acres of land for the Indian tribes as reservations (Johnson-Dodds 2002). This came to about 7.5% of the State of California. The California legislature argued against these treaties, taking the position that it would increase the conflict between the miners and the Native peoples of California (Johnson-Dodds 2002, Heizer 1974). According to the 1852 California Assembly Report of the Special Committee on the Disposal of Public Land:

> [I]t will be utterly impossible to prevent the collision between the miners and the Indians....it will be caused by the exclusive privileges attempted to be

> secured for Indians, to mines heretofore open to the
> labors of the white man. (Johnson-Dodds 2002: 23)

The treaties were not ratified by the U.S. Senate, and were held in secrecy until 1905 (Johnson-Dodds 2002).

In 1854, seven "military reservations" were set up on small areas of Federal land in California. These were "self-supporting work camps in which Indians would learn civilized skills and labor under white supervision," (Field 1999: 197). All but one of these were closed in the mid-1860s due to lack of funding and continued hostility from local white communities (Field 1999, Heizer 1978, Forbes 1982). During this time, Indians outside of these reservations were categorized as unrecognized by the federal government (Field 1999, Forbes 1982). These unrecognized groups made up the majority of Indians in California.

In the years 1906-1928, the Rancheria system was formed in California. These homesteads, many under 100 acres, were provided to "bands" or small groups of Indians (Field 1999, Forbes 1982). The creation of these Rancherias was a response to the deplorable conditions California Indians were living in. Their creation officially did not provide that the Indians had title or aboriginal rights to any land in the State (Field 1999). The federal Indian Agents working to establish these Rancherias used ethnographic authorities to define who the sociocultural groups that made up "bands" were. For instance, one of the agents, Charles E. Kelsey, drew on the work of C. Hart Merriam, Alfred Kroeber, and Stephen Powers (Field 1999).

However, not all the groupings identified to the BIA as sociocultural groups that warranted their own rancheria were given lands. Field (1999) notes that, Lafayette A. Dorrington, an Indian agent working under the authority of California, had gathered in 1927, a census of "homeless" sociocultural bands that were documented in the anthropological literature. But then,

> In the belief that the federal government should
> try to divorce itself from the responsibility for native
> groups, Dorrington would not say which groups
> needed land or housing, and therefore more than 100
> bands never received rancherias. [Field 1999:198, see
> also Dorrington 1927, Merrit 1927]

Field also notes that the anthropological literature of the time "minimized the cultural identities of many groups that appeared on the list and even claimed that some of them had become culturally extinct" (Field 1999:198). Field does not specifically mention the Juaneño as being one of the tribes that were so erased both by anthropologists and by Dorrington. However, the Juaneño did not receive a rancheria. Those tribes that did not receive rancherias during this time period thereby became "unrecognized" by the U.S. federal government.

The Juaneño-Acjachema have been seeking redress for this lack of recognition and other grievances from the federal and state governments since that time. In 1919, the Juaneño-Acjachema joined the Mission Indian Federation.[5] In meetings of this Federation, the Juaneño-Acjachema requested the U.S. federal government recognize them as a tribe and redress their grievances.

In 1928, the U.S. federal government finally attempted to meet the obligations laid out in the 1851 Treaties, specifically to give a cash award to American Indians native to California (Cook 1971). In order to do this, they needed to identify who the California Indians were, and so a census was conducted. Cook claims that the census was "correct in essence if not in minute detail" (1971a: 552). The total population of Indians in California according to the 1928 census was 23,542. This was the population for the state of California as a whole. County data for Orange, Los Angeles, and Riverside is as follows:

TABLE 2.1 AMERICAN INDIAN POPULATIONS BY COUNTY, 1860-1970 (ADAPTED FROM TABLE 5, PP 54-57; COOK 1976A):

County	1860	1870	1880	1890	1900	1905	1910
Los Angeles	2,014	219	316	144	69	-----	97
Orange*	----	----	-----	5	-----	-----	21
Riverside	-----	-----	-----	-----	809	-----	1,590

County	1920	1930	1940	1950	1960	1970
Los Angeles	281	997	1,378	1,671	8,109	24,509
Orange	990	125	66	134	730	3,920
Riverside	1,958	1,327	1,701	1,211	1,702	2,922

• Orange and Riverside were not separate counties until 1880.

5. From www.juanenoindians.com. The Mission Indian Federation was organized in 1919 and faded out in the 1930s, due to the economic conditions eroding participation. For more information in the Mission Indian Federation, see http://missionindianfederation.com.

Cook states that the early census had serious undercounts, due to American Indians tending to not cooperate with bureaucrats and government representatives. Discussing the early censuses, Cook notes that there were

> three primary defects of all the Federal census: First, the paid enumerators were too lazy or too incompetent to hunt out and visit all the known enclaves of Indian residents. Second, a great many Indians were sequestered in remote spots unknown even to reservation agents. Third, there was almost universal opposition to being interviewed by anyone with even a remote official association. Hence, even though bureaucratic policy might favor obtaining a full count, it was almost impossible to secure one in the field. (Cook 1976: 61)

Also, it must be noted that Orange and Riverside Counties were not in existence (as counties) before 1880, so there are no counts specific to these areas. Extrapolating from Mission reports and other data for Southern California Missions, Cook estimates a population of Southern California Mission Indians of 5,750 in 1870, a much higher number than the census count. The later censuses are likely somewhat more accurate. One must note the large jump for all the above counties for the 1970 census. This was during a time in which American Indians were beginning to become politically active. At this time it is very likely that people sought to explore their American Indian heritage, where previously they may have concealed it, or at the least minimized the importance of it.

People in the Juaneño-Acjachema community have told me that it was often the case that people actively hid or denied their Indian identity. The American Indian vagrancy laws of the 1850s were not repealed until 1937. Such laws being on the books, and a generation ago their being used to exterminate and enslave Indians, seems a fairly strong motivation to conceal one's American Indian identity. For minority groups, economic survival and success often requires a level of acculturation and even of "passing" as non-minority.

The 1970s was a time of political activism for many minority groups in the U.S. For American Indian tribes that did not have federal recognition, this was a time period especially marked by a resurgence of political activism and cultural resurgence. In the 1970s the federal government instituted a process through which unrecognized American Indian tribes could apply for federal recognition (officially called "acknowledgement"). This would formalize the relationship between the federal government and the tribe. It would also serve to legitimate the social claims of the tribe on American Indian identity. Juaneño are in no way unique in having their identity as Indian contested (see, for example, Blu 1980).

So in the 1970s, we see the formation of several American Indian organizations, and the beginnings of an outside-recognized organization of the Juaneño in San Juan Capistrano. In the next chapter, we will look at the process of petitioning for federal acknowledgement, and the Juaneño's experience with that process. That chapter will also examine Juaneño identity as it is "performed" in everyday life.

TABLE 2.2 TIMELINE OF KEY HISTORICAL EVENTS

DATE	HISTORICAL EVENT
1769	Gaspar de Portolá leads Spanish expedition up California Coast.
1776	Father Junipero Serra founds Mission San Juan Capistrano.
1806	The Great Stone Church completed after nine years of labor.
1812	Great Stone Church destroyed in earthquake of 1812, 42 killed.
1821	Mexico gains independence from Spain. San Juan Capistrano becomes Mexican territory. California provincial government decrees all missions in California should be secularized. Lands belonging to Mission San Juan Capistrano to be sold or given to private persons.
1833–1834	California Governor Jose Figueroa decrees secularization of the San Juan Capistrano Mission. All Acjachema at the Mission emancipated. They were given a little land. Setting up a *"pueblo de indios"* (Indian pueblo).
1841	Attempt to establish an "Indian Pueblo" at San Juan Capistrano Mission abandoned. Mission landholdings granted to Indian and non-Indian heads–of–households.

1845	Mission San Juan Capistrano sold at public auction. Purchased by John Forster and James McKinley.
1846–1848	U.S. – Mexican war.
1848	Treaty of Guadalupe Hidalgo. California becomes a U.S. Territory.
1849	Gold Rush begins: gold discovered in northern California, brings boom time to cattle industry in Southern California.
1850	California becomes a State. Los Angeles County includes territory that will become Orange County. First Federal Census of California.
1850	*An Act for the Government and Protection of Indians* (the California Indian vagrancy law) is enacted.
1852	Unratified Treaty of Temecula (Juaneños left out of Treaty). State census of California.
1853	California Indians confined to military reservations.
1862	Floods in Orange County, followed by smallpox epidemic, then drought. Cattle industry collapses, large ranchos are broken up.
1865	President Lincoln returns Mission San Juan Capistrano to the Catholic church.
1887	Railway built though San Juan Capistrano, connecting Los Angeles to San Diego.
1889	Orange County formed.
1906–1928	Rancheria system was formed in California. Juaneños not given a Rancheria.
1919–1921	Mission Indian Federation formed. Juaneños join.
1928–1933	Indians of California Claims rolls prepared.
1950	First Indians of California claims payment ($150).
1964	Second Indians of California Claims payment (about $650).

1978	Establishment of Federal Acknowledgement process.
1975	Capistrano Indian Council organized.
1978	Juaneño Band of Mission Indians organized.
August 17, 1982	Juaneño Band of Mission Indians, Acjachema Nation, file their Letter of Intent to Petition for Federal Acknowledgement with BIA.
Feb. 2, 1988	Juaneño Band of Mission Indians, Acjachema Nation, submits their Petition for Federal Acknowledgement.
Nov. 2007	BIA publishes Proposed Finding Against Federal Acknowledgement; Juaneño Band of Mission Indians, Acjachema given 180 days to respond.
March 15, 2011	Final Determination Against Federal Acknowledgement of the Juaneño Band of Mission Indians, Acjachema Nation (Petition 84A) and the Juaneño Band of Mission Indians (Petition 84B) is issued.

(Krekelberg, 2004, DOI 2007, Johnson-Dodds 2002, Orange County Historical Society 2010, PBS, 2010, Engelhardt 1922)

chapter 3

The Juaneño-Acjachema Today

American Indians in Southern California

American Indians in Southern California fall into two groups: members of tribes indigenous to the region, which include the Gabrieleño-Tongva, the Luiseño, and the Juaneño-Acjachema, and members of tribes indigenous to regions outside of southern California, who have migrated to Southern California. Those from outside Southern California vastly outnumber people from local tribes. The reasons for this are twofold. First, like those of all ethnic groups, many people of American Indian ethnicity came to Southern California for the weather, for opportunity, or because they were drawn by the Hollywood mystique. Secondly, during the 1950s, the U.S. Federal Government had a policy known as Relocation. In this program, American Indians who lived on reservations were encouraged and helped to move to urban locations, where they were given help in finding initial work and housing (Officer 1971). Los Angeles was the designated destination city for the Navajo Reservation Relocation Program, thus there are large numbers of Navajo in Southern California.

TABLE 3.1 RACIAL MAKEUP OF THE STATE OF CALIFORNIA

California Population	Number	Percent
Total population	37,253,956	100.0
RACE		
One race	35,438,572	95.1
White	21,453,934	57.6
Black or African American	2,299,072	6.2
American Indian and Alaska Native	362,801	1.0
Asian	4,861,007	13.0
Native Hawaiian and Other Pacific Islander	144,386	0.4
Some Other Race	6,317,372	17.0
Two or More Races	1,815,384	4.9

(Adapted from American Factfinder2 data retrieval: California; Race, Hispanic or Latino, Age, and Housing Occupancy: 2010; 2010 Census Redistricting Data (Public Law 94-171) Summary File)

Note that the above is for "one race," i.e. people who self-identified as only one race on their census form. When we include those who indicated that they were more than one race, the population of those who are American Indian or Alaska Native almost doubles, to 723,225, and is 6.6% percent of the total population of California.[1]

Most of the Juaneño-Acjachema live in Los Angeles, Orange, or Riverside Counties in California. American Indian populations in those counties range from 1.2% to 2% of the overall population.

---

1. See Appendix One for detailed mixed race census data.

TABLE 3.2 AMERICAN INDIAN OR ALASKA NATIVE
POPULATION OF CALIFORNIA, CENSUS 2010 DATA

Geographic area	American Indian or Alaska Native, single race	As single race, plus in any combination with other races	All races population	All AI/AN as % of total population
California	362,801	723,225	37,253,956	1.9%
Los Angeles County	72,828	132,196	9,818,605	1.3%
Orange County	18,132	37,582	3,010,232	1.2%
Riverside County	23,710	43,719	2,189,641	2%

(Adapted from: American Factfinder2; California; State & County Data; 2010 Census Redistricting Data)

TABLE 3.3 AMERICAN INDIAN AND ALASKA NATIVES IN SOUTHERN
CALIFORNIA (ALONE OR IN COMBINATION WITH OTHER RACES)

County	2005-2009 ACS data	2010 Census redistricting data	Amount of increase
Los Angeles County	116,578	132,196	15,618
Orange County	29,104	37,582	8,478
Riverside County	38,031	43,719	5,688
Tri-county Total	183,713	213,497	29,748

(People who self-identified as American Indian or Alaska Native alone, or in combination with one or more races, U.S. Census: American Community Survey 2005-2009 Estimates. 2010 Census Redistricting Data, Summary File, California: Race: Total Population)

Comparison of the 2005-2009 American Community Survey data and the 2010 Census redistricting data shows an increase in American Indian population across all counties. It is not clear whether this increase is due to higher birth rates, migration to the state of American Indians from other places, or an increase in ethnic self-identification as American Indians.

In the U.S. Census conducted in 2000, of those individuals across the U.S. who self-identified as belonging to tribes from Southern California there were: 1,810 Gabrieleño-Tongva, 3,370 Juaneño-Acjachema and 5,661 Luiseño.[2] Of the 3,370 Juaneño-Acjachema that are in the United States as a whole, 2,818 live in the state of California, and 2,132 live in the Los Angeles-Riverside-Orange CMSA[3] (Census Bureau 2000).

There are no American Indian enclaves or neighborhoods where Indians concentrate in Southern California. People in these communities, both those indigenous to Southern California and those who relocated here, maintain ties through family and social events, participation in cultural events like Pow Wows, basket-weaving groups, dance and music groups, and through participation in Indian specific social and governmental organizations, e.g. the Southern California Indian Centers, Inc., United American Indian Involvement, their own tribal governments, and American Indian churches.

San Juan Capistrano

San Juan Capistrano is the site of a historical Spanish Mission, the Mission San Juan Capistrano. It was through this Mission that the Acjachema people had their first documented contact with Europeans. It is the site of their original village, Putiidhem, and remains the emotional center of their community. For many generations it was a small town surrounded by ranches and orchards, and populated by Juaneño, Hispanics, and a minority of whites. It was still a small enough town during the 1950s, according to my informants who are old enough to have been giving birth at the time, that there was no doctor in residence. In the last fifty years what was once a small town has grown rapidly into a metropolitan area. The population of San Juan Capistrano as of the 2010 Census is 34,593. Of these, 77.1% are white, .6% are African-American, .8% are American Indian or Alaska Native, 2.8% are Asian, .1% are Native Hawaiian or other Pacific Islander, 15.1% indicated some other race than these, and 3.5% indicated they were more than one race.

---

2. As these are self-identifications, they reflect ethnic identity. These individuals may or may not be enrolled tribe members. Specific tribe identification is not reported in the more recent American Community Survey Data. At the time of this writing, 2010 census data reporting tribe affiliations has not been released.
3. Consolidated Metropolitan Statistical Area.

FIGURE 3.1 *Los Rios District in San Juan Capistrano.*

TABLE 3.4 SAN JUAN CAPISTRANO POPULATION, 2010

POPULATION	Number	Percent
Total population	34,593	100.0
RACE		
One race	33,385	96.5
White	26,664	77.1
Black or African American	193	0.6
American Indian and Alaska Native	286	0.8
Asian	975	2.8
Native Hawaiian and Other Pacific Islander	33	0.1
Some Other Race	5,234	15.1
Two or More Races	1,208	3.5

(Source: U.S. Census Bureau, Race, Hispanic or Latino, Age, and Housing Occupancy: 2010 Census Redistricting Data (Public Law 94-171) Summary File)

Southern California's County of Orange as a whole has seen tremendous growth and urbanization in this time period. Table 3.4 gives an idea of the growth of the region.

TABLE 3.5 ORANGE COUNTY POPULATION 1900-2010

Date	Orange County Population
1900	19,696
1910	34,436
1920	61,375
1930	118,674
1940	130,760
1950	216,224
1960	703,925
1970	1,420,386
1980	1,932,709
1990	2,410,556
2000	2,846,289
2009	2,976,831
2010	3,010,232

(1990-2000, census data, Census QuickFacts, 2009, 2005-2009 American Community Survey estimate; American Factfinder2, 2010 Census Redistricting Data, Summary File, California: Race: Total Population)

As the region has grown, the indigenous people have become more and more of a minority. Given the history of disenfranchisement, racism, outright attempts at eradication and elimination from the time of Spanish contact, it is not surprising that the Acjachema people sought to "blend into the background." Yet as the civil rights movements and the ethnic pride movements of the 1960s and 1970s saw some successes, being Indian was no longer something to be concealed. Many families and individuals sought to re-discover their American Indian identity. Concurrent with this was the political shift in which the Federal Government allowed for a formal process for groups to gain Federal Acknowledgement. This motivated the Juaneño in Southern California to seek to reestablish not only themselves individually as Indian, but to reestablish their tribe as a political entity.

However, as it became less dangerous to identify one's self as Indian, it also became, in the words of Paula Starr, executive director of the Southern California Indian Center, Inc., "cool to be Indian."[4] This raises a problem for those who are re-discovering their ethnic identity. They are at-risk for being accused of being "wanna-bes" and "New-Agers." These are non-Indian people who take on American Indian jewelry, dress, and practices. There are two processes at work here. One is the commodification of American Indian culture and spirituality. This is seen by some in the American Indian community as particularly egregious when it involves the sale of sacred items and the possibility of grave-robbing to acquire items. Also problematic is when whites seek to learn ritual practice from American Indian healers and practitioners, only to turn around and market themselves as healers of some kind. For many, such knowledge is to be held only by a few, and there are age and ritual restrictions on who may hold the knowledge. On the other hand, a brief walk through any Pow Wow or American Indian marketplace will reveal stall after stall selling dream-catchers, kachina dolls, and many other "sacred" objects. Most are being sold by American Indians. Clearly, the American Indian communities are not of one mind on this issue.

The second issue is the individual who does not just wear beaded earrings and have Zuni pottery in her household because she likes it, but who is passing herself off as American Indian. This is not a new phenomenon. In the 1920s in New York, there was a woman who called herself "Princess Chinquilla," who claimed to be of Cheyenne descent. Her identity as American Indian was challenged by many and investigated by American Indian activist Gertrude Simmons Bonnin (Carpenter 2005).

What does it mean to be American Indian?

All identity is negotiated and performed. West and Zimmerman (1987), in their discussion of "doing gender," state that gender is an "accomplishment," something that we engage in the creation of and the

---

4. Statement made to me while I was a graduate student research assistant, working on the American Indian Health Project, and the SCIC's Mobile Health Unit Project, in the early 2000s. I believe that this statement was very specifically directed at me, as a white person interested in American Indian issues, to caution me about being a "wanna-be," a white person who mimes American Indian jewelry, dress, and practices.

performance of, on a regular basis. In this performance, we constantly gauge the reaction of others, and will modify our behavior or "performance," if their reaction suggests we are not accomplishing the gender performance correctly. I suggest that American Indian identity is similarly performed. American Indians I observed while working in the American Indian community in southern California used several strategies to identify themselves to others as American Indian. They also, in some cases, took American Indian identity as a central feature of their life, and centered significant portions of their time, activities, and even at times their careers, around their American Indian identity.

For Juaneño-Acjachema people, performance of their American Indian Identity is particularly important. As a tribe without Federal Acknowledgement, without a reservation, without a "separate social space" that has not been encroached upon and "made white," they are in a near-constant struggle to prove themselves as American Indian, and in particular to prove themselves Juaneño.

Federal Acknowledgement

American Indians are a unique ethnic group in the United States in several ways. They are not a group that immigrated to the U.S., arriving as strangers to a new land. This was their land, and Europeans came as invaders. They are also a group that has a very particular legal relationship with the United States government. They are legally defined as Indian or not as individuals and as groups by the U.S. government. This brings us to the issue of the relationship between the federal government and American Indians, and to the issue of Federal Acknowledgement.

American Indians of Federally Acknowledged tribes have a special, legally defined relationship with the federal and state governments. This special relationship is due to their status as sovereign nations within the sovereign nation of the U.S. This status is based in original treaties negotiated by the U.S. government with the various American Indian tribes and governments, and has been modified and supported via other governmental acts, laws, statutes, and Supreme Court decisions.

It is important to understand this ongoing relationship not only because of the real practical effects it has on American Indian communities, but also because of how this relationship is viewed by American Indians. Many American Indians feel very strongly that they should be treated as sovereign nations. Most non-Indian Americans do not understand this government-to-government relationship, with the on-going obligations entailed in it, and feel that American Indians are getting some sort of special privileges that non-Indians are not getting.

The Legal Relationship

The relationship between the United States and American Indians began under British colonial rule. Two guiding principles of this interaction, which were maintained after U.S. Independence, were that (1) the Native American Indians had a compensable interest in the lands they occupied and used, and (2) that Indians required protection of the government (Officer 1971). The U.S. government acknowledged that American Indians should be compensated for the loss of their land, and originally set out that some of this compensation should be ongoing. It is important to understand that the seeking of Federal Acknowledgement and the benefits that come with it is not American Indians "looking for handouts" or some sort of welfare system. This is payment for their land. Moreover, it is not an unreasonable exchange, since the United States gained a great deal of land very cheaply. For example, from 1789 to 1850, via the negotiation and ratification of 245 treaties, the U.S. acquired more than 450,000,000 acres of land for less than $90 million (Officer 1971: 29).

Regarding the second principle, it became the policy that all dealings with American Indians, especially any land deals, go through the federal government, as local and state governments and individuals had habitually been party to the unfair treatment of Indians (Officer 1971).

The topic of American Indian law in its entirety is well beyond the scope of this book. However, in order to gain some basic understanding of tribal sovereignty and the nation-to-nation relationship between American Indian tribes (those that are Federally Acknowledged), a few key legal landmarks will be discussed. These include:

- The Northwest Ordinance of 1787
- The Constitution of the United States
- The Marshall Decisions (1831, 1832)
- The Trade and Intercourse Act of 1834
- The General Allotment Act of 1887
- The Indian Reorganization Act of 1934
- The House Concurrent Resolution 108 of 1953
- Public Law 280

The Northwest Ordinance of 1787

The Northwest Ordinance reads:

> The utmost good faith shall always be observed to-
> wards the Indians, their land and property shall never
> be taken from them without their consent; and in their
> property, rights and liberty, they never shall be invaded
> or disturbed, unless in just and lawful wars authorized
> by congress; but laws founded in justice and human-
> ity shall from time to time be made, for preventing
> wrongs being done to them, and for preserving peace
> and friendship with them. [Brophy et al 1966]

During this time following the U.S. Revolutionary War, the United States government dealt with American Indian tribes as foreign sovereign nations and made a concerted effort toward conciliation (Pevar 1992). The Northwest Ordinance reflects this. The Northwest Ordinance set a precedent for dealing with American Indians justly, and for compensating them for their lands.

U.S. Constitution (1789)

The Constitution is the basic authority for the conduct of Indian affairs. Article I, Section 8, the Commerce Clause, consigned to the federal government the power to regulate commerce with the Indian tribes (Brophy et al 1966, Svensson 1979). Jurisdiction over Indian land and relations with tribes were not to be carried out at the state level.

Up until the War of 1812, the U.S. government dealt rather cautiously with American Indians, in recognition of the fact that the Indians could easily trade alliances to other nations present on the continent, especially the French (Officer 1971). During this time, laws were enacted that protected American Indians in dealings with whites. For example, one wishing to trade with Indians must obtain a federal license, those who committed crimes against Indians could be prosecuted, and non-Indians were prohibited from settling on Indian lands (Pevar 1992). Unfortunately, these laws were generally not enforced.

Following the War of 1812, the U.S. had eliminated the threatening presence of the British to the north and the Spanish to the south. United States' Indian policy rapidly shifted toward Indian removal (Officer 1971, Champagne 1998). As will be seen below, this shift took on strength with the election of Andrew Jackson as U.S. president in 1828 (Pevar 1992). Jackson had been involved in numerous campaigns against American Indians in his military career; his position toward American Indians was unsympathetic. During Jackson's presidency, Indian policy focused on the removal of American Indians from lands east of the Mississippi to unsettled lands to the west (Pevar 1992). This applied to all Indians, even those who had "assimilated" to white civilization. Such was the case for the Cherokees and Choctaws of the Southeast. The Cherokee and Choctaw were landowners, farmers, and merchants. They spoke English, but were also literate in their indigenous languages. However, even with this level of assimilation, there were racial tensions between the Indians and their white neighbors (Sider 1993).

The Marshall Decisions

While the Cherokee were fairly assimilated, there were still race tensions in the state of Georgia. These came to a climax following the discovery of gold on Cherokee land. The state government of Georgia passed laws that distributed American Indian owned lands to the counties, voided all Indian law, and disallowed the legal testimony of Indians against whites (O'Brien 1989). These events led to a lawsuit that went to the Supreme Court, *Cherokee Nation v. Georgia*. This Supreme Court case was an examination of the legal status of the Indian in the United States. Georgia claimed that it was the right of the state to deal with American Indians, Cherokee claimed they were a foreign nation and that only the federal government had the right to make laws affecting them and their land. In 1831 Chief Justice Marshall ruled that the Cherokee were not a foreign nation as one is defined in the Constitution, but that they were a "domestic dependent nation" (O'Brien 1989). This definition left open the possibility that the Cherokee could gain the protection of the Federal government, while avoiding an open confrontation with President Jackson, who had said that he would remove the Cherokee regardless of how the Supreme Court ruled (O'Brien 1989).

However, this ruling left a great deal unclear. Another case was needed to clarify what was meant by "domestic dependent nation." Two missionaries, who were supporters and friends of the Cherokee nation, deliberately broke a Georgia law regulating residence on Indian lands (O'Brien 1989). This case, *Worchester v. Georgia*, was also taken to the

Supreme Court. Chief Justice John Marshall ruled that the Georgia laws were unconstitutional and interfered with treaties between the federal government and the Cherokee nation (O'Brien 1989). The ruling furthermore clarified "domestic dependent nation" as a protectorate relationship, and that it did not entail "individuals abandoning their national character, and submitting as subjects to the laws of the master," (O'Brien 1989: 58). In other words, while American Indian tribes were under the protection of the federal government, they maintained their status as sovereign nations. These judgments, often referred to as "the Marshall decisions," provided the foundation for all future federal-tribal relations (O'Brien 1989).

The Marshall Court ruled that the federal government had jurisdiction and that the state of Georgia and its citizens had no right to seize Indian lands. Unfortunately President Jackson neither respected nor upheld Marshall's decision (O'Brien 1989, Oswalt 1988). Eventually the Cherokee, Choctaw, and Creek were forced off their land and moved to Oklahoma in the well-known Trail of Tears.

The Trade and Intercourse Act

This Trade and Intercourse Act of 1834 restricted and defined who could make contracts with American Indians and regulated all business dealings with American Indians. Control of these matters was to be in the hands of the federal government, not the states (Pevar 1992, O'Brien 1989). Importantly, this Act provided that interests in Indian land, whether by lease or by purchase, could be acquired only by treaty or other agreement (Officer 1971). This Act is considered to have laid the framework for the operations of the Bureau of Indian Affairs, although that Bureau was created ten years earlier.

The Allotment Period: The Dawes Act

During the 1840s, the process of the removal of the majority of Indians from the eastern half of the U.S. was completed (Officer 1971). In 1849 the Bureau of Indian Affairs was transferred from the War Department to the Department of the Interior. This signaled a shift from dealing with Americans Indians militarily to dealing with them bureaucratically. Following the removal of Indians to the West was a period of the establishment of reservations via more treaty negotiations.

The goal of the U.S. federal government during this time period was assimilation of the American Indian into U.S. society. This was to be accomplished through the policy of allotment (Officer 1971). Congress passed the Allotment Act, or Dawes Act, as it was known in 1887, with amendments in 1891, 1906, and 1910. To many, the purpose of the Dawes Act was to break down American Indian culture and society, and force American Indians to assimilate to white lifestyles (Pevar 1992).

The Dawes Act authorized the president of the United States to parcel tribal land to individual members of tribes in tracts of 40, 80, or 160 acres, and was an extension of the 1875 Homestead Act (Brophy et al 1966, Officer 1971).

The allotments were held in trust by the federal government for twenty-five years. After that, they became privately owned by the individual or family they had been allotted to (Brophy et al 1966). Once the land became privately owned, the American Indian owner would become a U.S. citizen. The U.S. government would cease to have any special relationship with or obligations to the American Indians once they became U.S. citizens. Many have also interpreted this as them becoming "no longer Indian." The Secretary of Interior was to negotiate for the purchase of land leftover after all Indians had received a parcel, proceeds "were to be devoted to the education and civilization of the tribe," (Brophy et al 1966:19). The Dawes Act had little effect on California Indians, who at that time were largely landless (Field 1999).

The Dawes Act was supported by American Indian advocacy groups, many of whom were missionary and religious groups who had been working with Indians for some time (Officer 1971). The intention was to end the deep dependency that the reservation Indians had on federal rations since the Civil War and to free them from the deplorable conditions of the reservations (Officer 1971). The idea was that by giving them ownership of the land, they would take up farming and be self-supporting.

However, although many American Indians initially favored the policy, most had no training in farming or livestock raising. Moreover, the lands that were allotted to the Indians were of the poorest quality, and those "leftover" lands that were to be sold were those most suited to successful farming (O'Brien 1989). Also, most American Indians did not understand that once they owned the land, even though they owned it outright, they would have to pay taxes on it regularly. Once they attained individual ownership, many American Indians were then forced to sell the land because they could not pay the taxes (O'Brien 1989).

Under the operation of the Dawes Act, tribal landholdings were cut from approximately 138,000,000 acres to roughly 48,000,000 by 1934 (Officer 1971). It is one of the instances American Indians today will bring up as one of numerous attempts by the U.S. government to erase them as a people.

Concurrent in the development of allotment policies, and in alignment with a policy of promoting assimilation, was the development of an off-reservation boarding school system (Officer 1971). These schools removed Indian children from their homes, at times, forcibly. The children were often not allowed to speak their native language, were put into "white" clothing, had their hair cut, and suffered a regimented life. Many children subjected to the boarding school system did not return to their families at all (Officer 1971). Numerous people in the Juaneño community were sent to the Sherman Indian school in Riverside.

U.S. Citizenship

Prior to World War I, American Indians were only occasionally granted U.S. citizenship, and only then if they gave up their tribal citizenship (O'Brien 1989). Following the service of approximately 10,000 American Indian men in the First World War, a 1924 Act conferred citizenship on all American Indians who were not already citizens (Officer 1971, O'Brien 1989). This Act provided that this citizenship did not abrogate any rights they had as American Indians. Indians are currently citizens of three sovereign entities: the U.S. nation, their state, and their tribe.

The Meriam Report

A few years after the conferring of citizenship to American Indians, the U.S. government commissioned a study of the state and conditions of the American Indian (O'Brien 1989). The result of this study, the Meriam Report of 1928 documented the dire conditions of the life of American Indians, as well as the general disarray of federal policy to American Indians (O'Brien 1989). American Indians suffered from poverty, disease, and malnutrition: their life expectancy was 44 years of age, and their annual per capita income was one hundred dollars (O'Brien 1989:81). The Meriam report concluded that the health and education needs of American Indians were not being met by the BIA, and that American Indians were "being excluded from the management of their own affairs," (O'Brien 1989:81). It thus prompted the Indian Reorganization Act (O'Brien 1989, Officer 1971).

The Indian Reorganization Act

The Indian Reorganization Act, also known as the Wheeler-Howard Act of 1934, sought to repair the damage inflicted during the allotment era (Brophy et al 1966; O'Brien 1989, Officer 1971). The act:

- Stopped the alienation and allotment of Indian land
- Authorized appropriations to purchase new holdings for Indian use
- Established a system of federal loans to Indians to start businesses
- Confirmed Indian self-government
- Provided for the setting up of Tribal business organizations to be chartered as federal organizations
- Required Tribes accepting the Act to conserve their soil, water, timber, and vegetation resources
- Directed the Secretary of the Interior to inform Tribes of all estimates of the cost of federal projects for their benefit before submitting the figures to the Bureau of the Budget
- Made Indians eligible for BIA posts without regard to Civil Service laws; and established preferential hiring of Indians by the BIA.

Commissioner of Indian Affairs John Collier emphasized that this new Indian policy must end the "epoch of forced atomization, cultural prescription, and administrative absolutism," furthermore "there must be sought a cumulative involvement of all agencies of helpfulness. Federal, state, local, and unofficial" (Collier 1954:5, as quoted in Officer 1971: 44).

However, the O'Conner-Mundt House committee on Indian Affairs reported in 1944 that, "although the Wheeler-Howard Act (IRA) had in some instances aided the Indians, progress toward assimilation had lagged because of inadequate land, education, health guidance, and the government's failure to settle claims and to consolidate scattered holdings owned by several heirs" (Brophy et al 1966: 21).

House Concurrent Resolution 108: Termination

This resolution reversed most of the principles of the Indian Reorganization Act. The resolution sought to end the special relationship between the federal government and Indians (Officer 1971). But, Brophy et al notes:

> Indians, however, were already citizens by federal law, with all the rights possessed by their white neighbors. The term "wards" applied to them was, and had for a long time been, misleading. Except for the federal prohibitions against selling alcoholic liquor to Indians—repealed in 1953—they were subject to no greater federal control of their persons than any other citizens; they paid state and federal taxes the same as non-Indians, unless specifically exempted by treaty agreement or statute. Most of the exemptions applied only to real estate or income from trust property. [Brophy et al 1966:23]

Under this policy the Klamaths of Oregon in 1954 and the Menominees of Wisconsin in 1961, as well as a number of small tribes, lost their status as federally recognized Indians. By 1958 this policy had "lost much of its force," and by the 1970s tribes were no longer being terminated. Termination was later documented to have devastating effects on the health and welfare of the Klamath and the Menominees (O'Brien 1989). The Klamaths received restoration of federal recognition in 1986 (Klamath Tribe n.d.). The Menominees received restoration of federal recognition from Congress in 1973.[5] The policy of Termination was abandoned in large part due to the devastating effects it was seen to have on the tribes that were terminated. The Klamath and the Menominees both lost large portions of their land base, as well as federal funding for health and education. The loss of land made it more difficult to survive economically, and conditions deteriorated. The shift from Termination probably involved political processes as well. For example, President Nixon addressed Congress in 1970, calling for a shift in Indian policy that was toward "self-determination" rather than "forced termination" (Nixon 1970).

---

5. http://www.mpm.edu/wirp/ICW-104.html. Note that this was through an Act of Congress and not through the BAR process.

BIA Relocation Program

This program of off-reservation job training and placement of the 1950s and 1960s was "designed to relieve the pressure on reservation resources by assisting Indians to resettle" in off-reservation communities (Officer 1971: 45). Initially, there were placement offices located in Los Angeles, Phoenix, Denver, and Salt Lake City (Officer 1971). The program experienced expansion of funding and its programs throughout the 1950s. In 1956 an adult vocational training program was formed (Officer 1971: 49). The Relocation Program offered job training and assistance in relocating off the reservation and into urban areas. Health care was provided for relocating families through the private sector for six months after relocation.[6] During the 1950s and 1960s, the BIA relocated over 160,000 American Indians and Alaska Natives to cities across the United States.[7] This program was part of the cause of the migration of many Indians off-reservation, and a major factor as to why there are so many Navajo in Los Angeles. This project went hand-in-hand with Termination policies, seeking to move Indians into urban areas where it was expected they would integrate into Euroamerican lifestyles.

Public Law 280

Public Law 83-280, known as P.L. 280, gave civil and criminal jurisdiction to tribal lands and reservations in the states designated as "mandatory P.L. 280 states" in the law itself.[8] For mandatory states, no tribal consent was required to enact P.L. 280 (Goldberg 2004). Passed by Congress in 1953, it designated Alaska, California, Minnesota, Nebraska, Oregon, and Wisconsin as mandatory P.L. 280 states. Other states could choose to accept all or a portion of P.L. 280. States that have done so include: Arizona (1967), Florida (1961), Idaho (1963, for tribes that consented to it), Iowa (1967), Montana (1963), Nevada (1955), North Dakota (1963, for tribes that consented to it), South Dakota (1957-61), Utah (1971), and Washington (1957-63) (Goldberg 2004). After a 1968 amendment, only those tribes that consented would have P.L. 280 enacted and come under state jurisdiction (Goldberg 2004).

---

6. http://www.ihs.gov/NonMedicalPrograms/Urban/History.asp
7. http://www.ihs.gov/NonMedicalPrograms/Urban/History.asp
8. http://www.tribal-institute.org/lists/pl_280.htm

According to some viewpoints, Public Law 280 countered the Marshall decisions of 1831-32, which had respected the sovereignty of American Indian tribes. Public Law 280 did not affect the trust status of Indian lands nor was it supposed to affect the amount of BIA funds a tribe received. However, the BIA did use P.L. 280 as a reason to cut funds for education programs in California (Goldberg 2004).

There are, however, limitations to P.L. 280:

> States may not apply laws related to such matters as environmental control, land use, gambling, and licenses if those laws are part of a general state regulatory scheme. Public Law 280 gave states only law enforcement and civil judicial authority, not regulatory power. It also denied states power to legislate concerning certain matters, particularly property held in trust by the United States and federally guaranteed hunting, trapping, and fishing rights. The state cannot tax on the reservations. The United States Supreme Court has interpreted Public Law 280 as a statute designed to open state courts to civil and criminal actions involving reservation Indians, not to subject reservations to the full range of state regulation. (Goldberg 2004: § 6).

Thus, even while Public Law 280 is in effect in California, Indian Gaming can take place on reservations. Some note that P.L. 280 was a source of confusion and that it led to poor policing of reservation lands and little police protection for American Indians on the reservation (Darian-Smith 2004).

Federal Acknowledgement

In 1978, the United States federal government specified the criteria for Recognition of a Tribe by the Federal Government. This differs from being recognized *as American Indians.* It can be the case that individuals are recognized as Indians, *but not as a tribe with whom the federal government has made treaties* and thus has ongoing obligations to. This is a key point for the Juaneño-Acjachema, as many individuals in the tribe have cards from the Bureau of Indian Affairs that identifies them as Indian.

The kinds of obligations due to Federal Acknowledgement have shifted through time, but now are primarily the provision of health-care, land, and financial support for education.[9] One of the major goals of the Juaneño people who spoke with me about this was to get land for the tribe. Following Federal Acknowledgement, the tribe would be given grant money to purchase anywhere in their historical territory. Many hoped that this could be used for a cultural center or museum. Of course, the possibility that a casino could be built on such a property has been the source of much controversy, and was a factor in at least one of the political rifts the tribe experienced in the 1990s.

Many American Indian tribes, including the Juaneño, are in the process of seeking Federal Acknowledgement. This process is conduct-ed through a Petition for Federal Acknowledgement that is sent to the Office of Federal Acknowledgment, a subdivision of the U.S. Depart-ment of the Interior's Bureau of Indian Affairs.[10]

The federal requirements to qualify for Acknowledgement, which are located in Part 83.7 of Title 25 of the Code of Federal Regulation state:

§ 83.7 Mandatory criteria for Federal Acknowledgment:

a) The petitioner has been identified as an American Indian entity on a substantially continuous basis since 1900.

b) A predominant portion of the petitioning group comprises a dis-tinct community and has existed as a community from historical times until the present.

c) The petitioner has maintained political influence or authority over its members as an autonomous entity from historical times until the present.

d) A copy of the group's present governing document including its membership criteria [must be submitted]. In the absence of a written document, the petitioner must provide a statement de-scribing in full its membership criteria and current governing procedures.

e) The petitioner's membership consists of individuals who de-scend from a historical Indian tribe or from historical Indian tribes which combined and functioned as a single autonomous political entity.

9. See the Bureau of Indian Affairs website for more information regarding the tasks and activities of the BIA. www.bia.gov
10. Office of Acknowledgement: www.bia.gov/WhoWeAre/AS-IA/OFA/index.htm

f) The membership of the petitioning group is composed principally of persons who are not members of any acknowledged North American Indian tribe.

g) Neither the petitioner nor its members are the subject of congressional legislation that has expressly terminated or forbidden the federal relationship.

[25 CFR Ch. I (4–1–08 Edition)[11]]

The process of the Juaneño-Acjachema petitioning for Federal Acknowledgement has been documented by the Bureau of Indian Affairs in their published Proposed Finding (DOI 2007b). The Juaneño Band of Mission Indians, Acjachemem Nation (JBMI) submitted a Letter of Intent to Petition for Federal Acknowledgement on August 17, 1982, beginning the process. Not surprisingly, given the extensive list of criteria above, it took some time before they were able to submit their full petition. This was submitted on Feb. 2, 1988, and the petition then received the designation of Petition 84A. After an initial Technical Review that assisted the tribe in the process, the BIA placed the petition on the "ready list" in September of 1993. However, that summer, there was a tribal election that was disputed by some members of the tribe, leading to a factioning of the tribe. Sonia Johnston claimed to have been elected, and when she was not designated the winner of the election, she split from the group, taking some members with her. This group, calling itself, "The Juaneño Band of Mission Indians," (JBB) then submitted their own petition in March of 1996, which the BIA designated petitioner 84B. At this time David Belardes was the leader of Juaneño Band of Mission Indians, Acjachemem Nation (petition 84A).

Following this split, the groups notified the BIA that they would be submitting revised membership lists. According to the BIA, as stated in their Proposed Finding of 2007, since the membership lists are part of the petition process, the group was no longer ready to be considered and was removed from the ready list (DOI 2007). Following submission of a revised membership list, the two groups were put back on the ready list in February of 1996. However, they were placed at the bottom of the list, where they had been close to the top before. It would be another nine years before they actually came under consideration.

---

11. Available online at: http://edocket.access.gpo.gov/cfr_2008/aprqtr/pdf/25cfr83.7.pdf

According to informants in the community, part of the political tensions in the JBMI arose from the fact that when they were close to consideration for Federal Acknowledgement, the leadership of the tribe was approached by investors interested in facilitating the tribe opening a casino. The tribe was divided about whether this was a good idea or not. In April of 1997, there was another disputed election in the JBMI. Jean Frietze was elected as tribal chair (DOI 2007). David Belardes, the outgoing tribal chair, dis-enrolled himself from the tribe, and formed a third faction. In their proposed finding, the BIA refers to Belardes and his group as an "interested party."[12]

In 2005, with Anthony Rivera as Tribal Chair, the JBMI submitted a new set of materials to the Office of Acknowledgement (OFA). They were placed on active consideration in September of 2005. In November of 2007, the BIA published a Proposed Finding Against Acknowledgement. For both groups, designated Petition 84A and 84B, the Bureau of Acknowledgement report stated that they did not satisfy criteria 83.7(a), 83.7(b), 83.7(c), and 83.7(e).

This was not the end, however. The tribe was given 180 days to respond. They submitted more materials in support of their petition, and were told they would be given a Final Determination by June of 2010. The Office of Federal Acknowledgement then extended this to September 30, 2010. Then they extended it to December 15, 2010, and again to February 15, 2011.

On March 17, 2011, there was a Press Release from the Department of the Interior (DOI) stating that the Juaneño Band of Mission Indians, Acjachema Nation (JBMI, in DOI publications JBA, petition 84A) and the Juaneño Band of Mission Indians (JBB, petition 84B) had received their Final Determination, and that both groups were denied Federal Acknowledgement. The Notice Letter reiterated the criteria not met as noted in the Proposed Finding of November 2007, as follows, in the press release for petition 84A (JBMI):

> The four criteria the petitioner does not meet are Criteria 83.7(a), 83.7(b), 83.7(c) and 83.7(e).

> Criterion 83.7(a) requires that external observers have identified the petitioner as an American Indian entity

---

12. Research for this book involved little contact with members of this faction. This however, is not intended to lend legitimacy to one faction over another.

on a substantially continuous basis since 1900. The available evidence demonstrates that external observers identified the petitioner as an American Indian entity on a substantially continuous basis only since 1997, not since 1900.

Criterion 83.7(b) requires that a predominant portion of the petitioning group has comprised a distinct community from historical times to the present. The available evidence demonstrates that the distinct SJC Indian community, from which the petitioners claim descent, continued to exist only to 1862.

Criterion 83.7(c) requires that the petitioning group has maintained political influence over its members as an autonomous entity from historical times to the present. The available evidence does not demonstrate that the petitioner maintained political influence or authority over its members as an autonomous entity from 1835 until the present.

Criterion 83.7(e) requires that the petitioner's members descend from a historical Indian tribe. The available evidence shows that only 61 percent of the petitioner's 1,940 members demonstrated descent from the historical Indian tribe at San Juan Capistrano Mission. [DOI 2011a]

The press release for 84b differs only in the statement regarding 83.7(e):

The available evidence shows that only 53 percent of the petitioner's 455 members demonstrated descent from the historical Indian tribe at San Juan Capistrano Mission. [DOI 2011b]

The process allows for an appeal of the Final Determination. Leadership of the Juaneño Band of Mission Indians, Acjachema Nation has stated that they will appeal the finding.

Juaneño-Acjachema Ethnic Identity

Race Science

In 1758, Carolus Linnaeus, in his *Systema Naturae*, which is a taxonomy of all life forms, identified variations of *homo sapiens*, variations of skin color, hair type, and other physical features, which were then linked to personality types, habits, and customs (Gould 1996). Biology was used as an explanation of human social and cultural variation. The idea that there are sub-groupings of human beings which are biologically different from each other has been a part of Western cultural ideas since that time, even with overwhelming genetic evidence that no such biological sub-groups exist (Gould 1996).

Race categories must be understood in the historical context of the imperial conquest and enslavement of non-white peoples worldwide. The creation of the idea of biological groups, and the linkage of social and personality traits to those groups, is part of the hegemonic process of creating a story in which one group is superior to all others. The supposed biological inferiority of non-whites has been used to justify their conquest, enslavement, and oppression. It has been used to rationalize the impoverished conditions of many non-whites, their poor school performance, and lower median incomes. In other words, it has been used as a curtain to hide the deep racial stratification of our society both today and in the past.

Yet, the idea of a biological reality of American Indian identity is often a part of how American Indians view themselves, as well as how they are viewed by the U.S. Bureau of Indian Affairs. There are requirements to document genealogy for both individuals and groups to be "legitimately American Indian." Individuals can submit genealogical evidence to the BIA and get a card that says not only that they are Indian, but what their "blood quantum" is: what percentage of "Indian blood" they are. Genealogical descent gets represented through the metaphor of blood. This idea of being "part Indian" is something many American Indians struggle with.

Given this history of the construction of ethnicity ("race") as biological, it is surprising that I heard little discussion during my fieldwork of how Indian someone was based on their physical appearance. This has been noted for some other American Indian groups as well. Blu (1980) notes that the Lumbee also do not speak of who is and who is not Indian in terms of physical appearance, but in terms of behavior and speech. The Lumbee, indigenous to what is now North Carolina, are also a tribe that struggled for both Federal Acknowledgement and recognition by others, Indians and whites, of their Indian identity. During the early 1800s the Lumbee were legally designated "Free Persons of Color" (Sider 1993). Since then they have gone through various contestations over their origins, and over "what Indians they were." They have now been legally acknowledged by the federal government as Lumbee, but with the very important clause in this legal acknowledgement that such acknowledgement entails no legal obligation to the Lumbee by the federal government (Blu 1980:88).

Social Construction of Ethnic Identity

Anthropologists have characterized American Indian ethnic identity as a social construction (Nagel 1994, Sanders 2002). This view considers "the ways in which ethnic boundaries, identities, and cultures, are negotiated, defined, and produced through social interaction inside and outside of ethnic communities" (Nagel 1994: 152). The Juaneño-Acjachema are in a continual state of "negotiation" of who is and who is not legitimately Juaneño. Since the early 1990s, when the Juaneño-Acjachema appeared to be close to consideration of their application for Federal Acknowledgement, this process has intensified. Juaneño identity is negotiated in part through genealogy, which the Juaneño Band of Mission Indians, Acjachema Nation (JMBI) aided individuals in researching. This process was in some ways undermined when in the Proposed Finding of 2007, the BIA specifically named individuals whom they designated as not Juaneño-Acjachemem. Some of these were designated by the BIA as not Indian at all, some were designated as "Mission Indians" but not Juaneño. The leadership of the JBMI then had to go through the very difficult process of dis-enrolling individuals and families who were designated by the BIA as not Juaneño. Had they not done this, they would have been unable to continue with the petition for Federal Acknowledgement. This was traumatic for the community as well as for the individuals and families involved, leaving many with hurt feelings and anger toward the leadership of the JBMI.

The negotiation of identity happens on a daily basis through many aspects of individual's lives, and few ethnic groups experience the legal definition of their identity through a government bureaucracy. In this next section of the chapter I will discuss some of the ways I observed Juaneño-Acjachemem people negotiating their identity as American Indian and as specifically Juaneño-Acjachema in their day-to-day lives.

Who is "really Indian"?

In the seven years that I worked in American Indian communities in Southern California, I heard almost constant contestations and discussion over who is and who is not "really Indian." These debates often fell along a number of lines:

(1) You are not Indian if you did not grow up on a reservation.
(2) You are not Indian if you are Mexican.
(3) You are questionable if you claim to be Cherokee.

The assessment of one as "not Indian" when they claim Cherokee has a basis in the fact that the Cherokee Nation has a low "degree of Indian blood" requirement for tribal membership. While working as a graduate student research assistant on the American Indian Health Project,[13] which brought me into contact with American Indians throughout Southern California, not just Juaneño, I often encountered the Cherokee reference as a kind of joke. Someone claimed to be Indian, but was suspect, and someone would say, "oh, they're *Cherokee*." Such a statement was often followed by a laugh or an eye-rolling gesture.

The association with, or identification of oneself as in any way Mexican was a basis for negation of American Indian identity. At one point I was at a reunion of one of the Juaneño factions, sitting with a group of women at a campground. One of the women glanced across the campground at another group at the reunion and commented disparagingly, "those Mexicans." The clear implication was that they were therefore not legitimately Acjachema. This assessment of one or another as "Mexican" was commonplace in the discussion of the various political factions about each other, in attempts to de-legitimize the other group. Considering the Southwest and California were a part of Mexico up until 1848, this is an interesting facet of American Indian identity. The ethnicity "Mexican" is in itself a mix of Spanish and indigenous historical populations. It is interesting that these have come to be oppositional categories in the social construction of who is and who is not Indian.

13. The American Indian Health Project was at that time being conducted out of University of California at Irvine's Center for Health Policy and Research, Dr. Laura Williams, Principal Investigator.

Living on, or being linked to a reservation is also a part of legitimacy of American Indian identity. The Juaneño are not federally recognized, and have no trust land, or reservation land, that is theirs. So the Juaneño are not "reservation Indians," and are thus "questionably Indian." They also do not have an ethnic enclave, a community that is cleanly separate from non-Indian communities. Also, for those American Indians who experienced reservation life, there is this idea of the experience of hardship as part of American Indian identity. Impoverishment is an aspect of American Indian identity, even if that impoverishment is in the past, as is the case for those few American Indian groups who have been successful with casinos. This linking of impoverishment and the associated suffering of the impoverished and American Indian ethnic identity is not unique to this community or study (cf Carpenter 2005).

Darian-Smith (2004) points out, in her discussion of California Indians and casinos, that "rich Indians" are seen as "inauthentic" in their Indian identity. One member of the Juaneño-Acjachema community that I worked with is rather successful and has a good income. In talking to her after a Juaneño Band of Mission Indians, Acjachema Nation General Council meeting, we walked to her car, which was parked in the back of the parking lot. It was a new Mercedes, a brand generally associated with wealth and success. I commented on the car, and she said that it was a good car, but that we wouldn't mention it to the people in the tribe. So, this car, which in mainstream America is a symbol of wealth and success, and would usually be displayed prominently, is hidden rather than shown off.

Stereotypes

In the social sciences, we often talk about stereotypes, and the negative effects of stereotypes on people, particularly ethnic minorities. American Indians are one such group, with lots of stereotypes about them in existence and still in the majority cultures' discourse. Yet, while stereotypes can be damaging, many of the American Indians I observed used these stereotypes to enact and perform their identity as American Indians.

American Indians are sometimes stereotyped as "primitive," or, with a less negative connotation, as closer to nature than whites. This characterization has associated ideas of spirituality and environmentalism (Darian-Smith 2004, Carpenter 2005). This stereotype is often based in the belief that their governments and subsistence strategies pre-colonially were more sustainable and ecologically sound than our industrial economic system.

American Indians, Juaneño and others, often talk about themselves as being closer to the land, as understanding nature, and even as having some special skill for communicating with animals. So the prevalent stereotypes of American Indians are not simply imposed on them by others, and they are not simply a mode of oppression. They are actively used by American Indians in the presentation of self and negotiation of identity.

Some even use this stereotype as a means of income. For example, the horse trainer GaWaNi Pony Boy, promotes "Native American Horsemanship." In the Introduction to his book, *Horse Follow Closely*, he makes explicit links between good horsemanship—here characterized as Native American Horsemanship—and environmental concerns:

> If we are to understand our relationship with the horse, we must first understand the relationship we have with the entire animal kingdom. The human species, directly or indirectly, affects all other species on the planet, even those species we don't directly come into contact with. Every one of our actions affects all living things, and therein lies our responsibility to the natural world. Native Americans understood this. They held at their core the belief that all species are related. They also understood that a certain level of awareness must take place before we can truly communicate with that which is around us. (Pony Boy 1998:1)

Like most of the majority culture in the United States, GaWaNi Pony Boy here refers to "Native Americans" as if they are one people and one culture. The indigenous peoples of the United States, both before European contact and now, are made up of many cultures and languages, with different traditions, religions, and historically different political systems and subsistence strategies. Also, the horse was introduced rather late into the Americas, and although a number of tribes took up the horse and used it to their advantage, to the best of my knowledge the Cherokee, which is Pony Boy's tribal affiliation, were not one of them. So here we have a specific case of someone, quite successfully, using his Native American identity to promote himself. For while GaWaNi Pony Boy is very likely a good horse trainer in his own right, a great deal of the draw of his clinics and books comes from the "Native American" angle. And this angle is by no means downplayed. The book quoted from above is filled with beautiful pictures of Pony Boy and his horse, he is in buckskins, his face painted, his horse painted, and is often photographed riding bareback with only a rope through his horse's mouth. Interestingly, in the sections showing actual training sessions, he does use a side-pull or snaffle bridle. Many of the photographs are in settings that look to be in the Southwestern U.S.; one has him posed in front of a Tipi. Cherokee were not from the Southwest, and definitely did not use Tipis. The drawing on of the American stereotypes of "what an Indian is" is starkly clear.

This is hardly the only example of Native Americans using the stereotypes that abound about them to make their living. One has only to walk through the New-Age section of any bookstore to find numerous examples of American Indians using their image of themselves as "spiritual" and "connected to natural things" and therefore able to provide spiritual guidance or life advice.

I am not sure if this is a negative or a positive, and it may well be some of both. The ownership of an American Indian identity in a public way can be a good thing after many years of being ashamed and, according to people I have spoken to, hiding their Indian-ness. The growth of the stereotype of the "natural" and "spiritual" American Indian has been concurrent with the growth of the New Age movement in the United States. The New Agers have, in many instances, appropriated Native American imagery and practices. The American Indian community as a whole has not appreciated this. For many American Indian tribes, sacred knowledge is to be held only by a few specific people, not published for general reading or used by some (often non-Indian) individual for monetary profit. Furthermore, Juaneño community leaders report problems with people grave-robbing: going to places that are sacred sites, where people are buried, to take items to use in their own "spiritual practice."

American Indian culture has become a commodity. One can buy items of American Indian jewelry, craft, clothing, home decorations, and food, drink, and herbal remedy items. One can buy books teaching you how to practice American Indian spirituality, or practices that are not Native American Indian, but make use of images and symbols associated with Native Americans. For example, Tarot cards with pictures of eagles, bears, and feathers, are marketed as an American Indian spiritual practice. This commodification of Native American Spirituality "den[ies] the very existence of traditional Native American beliefs as valid ways of life today. They do not foster Native American lifestyles—they trivialize them" (Wesaw 1995: 10).

In the Juaneño-Acjachema community, this played out in various ways. At times, in the community health projects I was involved in, I had the opportunity to attend meetings and community health education programs. These were often held in parks or campgrounds. The sites were important not only in that they were a natural setting, but many were also historically important: village sites and ceremonial sites. These events usually combined biomedical health education and culturally significant healing practices. For example, one community health education event was a retreat held over a weekend at a rural mountain campground. During the day were discussions of healthy food choices and the need to get breast cancer screenings, and at night there was a ceremonial Bear Dance.

At another community meeting, also being held outside in a park-like setting, a bird was singing overhead. A woman was speaking, she pauses, turns toward the bird and says, "I hear you," suggesting that she had some particular understanding of the bird, and that the bird's purpose was to specifically communicate with her. The public nature of her doing this cannot go unremarked: she already had the attention of the group, as she was saying something in the group meeting, and says aloud her "communication" with the bird. A declaration of her connection with nature, her Indian-ness, and her spirituality.

Presentation of Self

Goffman (1959) focuses on one's identity as acted out in social interactions and in one's presentation of themselves, i.e., one's clothing, hairstyles, body decorations, the objects one carries. Among the Juaneño people I worked with, I noticed that these things often incorporated American Indian themes and symbols. Here I saw a great deal of use of pan-Indian symbols: symbols which have come to be associated with Indians generally, when they originated with a specific tribe.

For example, women will often wear beadwork. This can appear as jewelry or be stitched into clothing. Very often this is subtle, not a full regalia or even all items of clothing as American Indian, but perhaps jeans, a sweatshirt, and beadwork earrings, or a bit of beadwork on the pocket of the jean jacket. This might be beadwork the woman has done herself, or it might have been purchased. Another example is the use of images and animals associated with American Indians. T-shirts and sweatshirts are often adorned with images of eagles, wolves and horses, and often with feathers or stylistic graphics.

Why do Juaneño use Pan-Indian symbolism? Pan-Indian refers to symbols that have come to represent American Indians generally. Most are drawn from specific tribes, like the feather headdress of a chief, tipi, and Paint horse that come from plains tribes. Some are animals that have come to be associated with American Indians, like the wolf and the eagle.

Why wear dream-catcher earrings, when dream catchers are a Navajo artifact? While some might claim that this is because the Juaneño-Acjachema "no longer have their own culture," this is neither true nor the reason, I think, why so much pan-Indian symbolism is used.

Consider Goffman's idea of dramaturgy (1959), that people are "on-stage" in their daily lives. In this, Goffman considers the "presentation of self" that one engages in: one's dress, body decoration, and even the "props" one might carry. Thus, a business person would wear a suit, carry a briefcase, and have a high-end cell phone to identify him- or herself as a business person. Moreover, in non-office public places, like a coffee shop, he would very likely be on the cell phone, loudly discussing business, so that everyone present is made aware the he is a business person, and is working hard. This individual is wearing the "costume" of the business person, has the props, and performs a role publically that reflects social ideas of what business people do, and supports the capitalist value of constant work (he cannot really stop for coffee, he must work while doing even that). Similarly, the American Indian person can be considered through dress, props, and behavior to be presenting herself as American Indian. For the Juaneño this becomes especially important in that her identity is so often contested, and that other means of identifying herself as American Indian, like Federal Acknowledgement or linkage to a reservation, is not readily available to her. The Juaneño, in their choice of "costuming" and "props" often choose pan-Indian symbols. Why?

In any real stage performance, one of the basic rules is this: don't confuse your audience. This also holds for social "role performance." If one wishes to identify oneself as American Indian to the general public, then one had better use symbols that the general public associates with American Indians. So, while the California condor is an important bird in traditional Juaneño-Acjachema ritual practice, wearing a picture of one on a sweatshirt would be unlikely to be recognized by the general public as associated with American Indian-ness. But, if you wear a sweatshirt with a picture of an eagle, add some recognizable Navajo or Zuni graphic designs, you have made your point. Your audience understands your costume. Moreover, you might be hard-pressed to find a sweatshirt with a California condor on it. So here the commodification of American Indian culture facilitates the presentation of self as American Indian.

Public Performance of Juaneño-Acjachema Identity

I attended many public events, meetings, and ceremonies during the time I worked with the Juaneño-Acjachema. Usually, when someone gets up to speak, they do not just simply identify themselves by name, but they will identify lineage: name the families that they are descended from, and at times even tie themselves to a particular location. Sometimes one might link themselves to a particular village-site ("My ancestors trace themselves back to this village of Panhe, as found in the Mission baptismal records") sometimes they tie themselves to the historic district in San Juan Capistrano: "My family is the _____ and the _____'s who lived in the Rios District here in Capistrano."

Other times the individual did not (or did not only) identify themselves as legitimately Juaneño through their naming of lineage, but by use of the Juaneño language. The Juaneño language is not regularly spoken by anyone today. However, there was documentation of the language by the anthropologist Harrington. So people can learn some of the language, and at times people get together in class-like situations to do just this. Many times, an individual will memorize a prayer to say at public events, often a translation of the Christian Lord's Prayer into Juaneño. So the individual recites a prayer in the Juaneño language, thus presenting themselves as legitimately Juaneño. They also are thus identifying as Catholic. Many Juaneño I met were strongly Catholic. Others pointed out the role the Catholic church had in the colonization of the Juaneño-Acjachema people, and have nothing to do with the church.

One's household can be seen as an extension of themselves and thus of their identity performance. I cannot think of one American Indian home that I was in that did not have some aspect of the décor that incorporated American Indian imagery. To be clear, these were households in urban and suburban southern California, that in all other ways were like the homes of their neighbors. But they were adorned with a variety of items of Native American symbols: pottery, kachina dolls, artwork of profiles of American Indians, of eagles and wolves, dream-catchers as wall-hangings, and Pendleton rugs as couch throws.

Again, for the Juaneño, most of these were Pan-Indian symbols. Some notable exceptions were one family who had a replica of a kiicha (traditional Acjachemem house) on their front lawn. Others also had some household décor that was Juaneño-specific: Acjachemem basketry or basket-weaving samples, acorns, and rabbit furs.

In 2010, while writing this book, I visited the home of a Juaneño woman who had been one of the informants for the research project. In discussing some recent political developments in the tribe and her frustration with them, she said: "I'm not Indian anymore." She then pointed out that she had taken down all the American Indian artwork, the table-top she had in the past that had been covered in skins, furs, kachina dolls, Native American pottery, shells, and where even an American Indian Barbie had been on display. Here we have it explicitly stated: her identification as American Indian is in part expressed by her house décor. She takes down the American Indian artwork and is "no longer Indian."

Occupation

Some individuals made a career choice because of their Native American identity. Jacquie Nunez, for example, owns and operates a business called Journeys to the Past. In this business, she gives performances at elementary schools educating students about the Acjachema people. She also holds summer camps at the San Juan Capistrano Mission.

Some individuals go into service positions that specifically serve the American Indian community. For example, Sonia Johnston, leader of the JBB group at the time of data collection, then worked at the Southern California Indian Centers, Inc, helping to coordinate access to social services for American Indian people.

I asked women I interviewed and who responded to the questionnaire what they did or participated in as part of their American Indian identity. Many women talked about hobbies and crafts they participated in: basket-weaving, beading, carving and decorating gourds. One of the regular community activities I participated in was a weekly basket-weaving group that was held at the JBMI tribal office at that time. Generally for senior ladies, other age groups (and even the occasional man) participated. Now here was another example of being more "pan-Indian" than Juaneño. For the most part, the ladies in the basket-weaving class did a kind of basketry known as "Cherokee." This is a fairly simple form of basket-weaving. One can learn it fairly quickly, and if someone has made a "start" for you (the beginning of the basket, which is the hardest part), you can complete a basket in about a half-hour. Materials used are generally reed, which can be purchased at a local store that sells weaving materials.

Traditional Juaneño-Acjachema basketry, on the other hand, is very different. These are coiled baskets, a process that takes a great deal of skill, practice, and manual dexterity. Not to mention patience. A me-

dium-sized basket entails hundreds of hours of work. The traditional materials are deer grass and juncus. These materials must be gathered from local wilderness areas, and then carefully dried and processed to become usable for weaving. It is not surprising that most people do not make these types of baskets. In the time I did my research, the only person I knew of who could successfully carry out the traditional Juaneño basketry is a non-Juaneño man named Abe Sanchez. He makes a consid-
erable effort to teach

FIGURE 3.2 *Abe Sanchez at the Earth Day at Panhe event, where he is demonstrating foods from local plants.*

Juaneño-Acjachema people traditional basket-weaving. Many do try, but most do not make these traditional baskets on a regular basis due to the high skill level involved and the difficulty of getting materials.

Many Juaneño women do "pine-needle" baskets. This is coiled basketry with a pine-needle base for the coils, with the coils or needles stitched together with raffia or heavy cord thread, or in one case I was shown, a sinew thread. This comes closer to traditional Juaneño basketry, but is still criticized as "not traditional."

Preservation of Land

Given that there is this idea of American Indians as closer to nature than whites, it is not surprising that many American Indian people are interested in preservation of land and environmental concerns. For some Juaneño-Acjachema people, the fight to preserve a piece of land is not only about environmental concerns, but is about preserving specific sites that are of historical and spiritual significance. Many sites are known through archaeological evidence, written historical evidence, and oral history to be village sites, burial sites, or sites where specific religious ceremonies took place. A few of these sites have managed to escape development (a surprising fact in the sprawling suburbia of Orange County, California). However, the sites are under constant threat of development. Many Juaneño-Acjachema work diligently to preserve these sites. Organizations that aid in this work include the California Cultural Resources Preservation Alliance (www.ccrpa.com), and the United Coalition to Protect Panhe. The California Cultural Resources Preservation Alliance is composed of scientists, American Indian People, and advocates of land preservation. They fight development of American Indian sacred and historical sites throughout California. The United Coalition to Protect Panhe grew out of the fight to protect the Panhe village site in San Clemente (San Mateo Campgrounds) from a toll road that was slated to be extended through the area. Working with other organizations, like the Sierra Club and the California State Parks Foundation, the group succeeded in blocking the toll roads construction through the Panhe site in December of 2008.

The Ancestors Walk described in the opening of this book was started as an effort to make people aware of the need for the preservation and protection of historically, spiritually, and culturally important sites in Southern California. This event was started by Lilian Robles, a woman of mixed Juaneño-Acjachema and Gabrieleño-Tongva descent, who is probably best known for her role in the preservation of the PaVungna site on the campus of California State University at Long Beach. In 1993 the University wanted to build a strip mall on what had been a community garden on the campus (Harper 2006). This land was the site of the believed emergence of Chinigchinich (Harrington 1934). Lillian Robles began a vigil on the land, bringing her sleeping bag and tent, she stayed on the land to prevent the University from developing (Harper 2006). She was soon joined by others, and the land was eventually saved from development. Lillian Robles went on to fight for the preservation of other sites, and along with Jimi Castillo, a Gabrieleño-Tongva/Juaneño-Acjachema spiritual leader, started the Ancestors Walk in 1997.

This chapter examined the ways in which Juaneño-Acjachema identity is negotiated and performed. The legal and social aspects of this are things that Juaneño-Acjachema people deal with on a daily basis. The next chapter deals with Juaneño-Acjachema identity as it influences reproductive practices. In the passing on of childbirth beliefs and practices, mothers teach their daughters not only to ensure the health of their children on the way, but also to ensure that they are Acjachema people.

chapter 4

The Reproduction of People and Culture

They had a custom that the first time that the woman found herself pregnant, all the people of the rancheria held a feast, eating and dancing, and this for one night only. This feast was held with the rejoicing that another one was coming to them, and in the song of the dance, they asked their God Chinigchinix to guard for them that child. (Harrington 1934: 26)

My research with Juaneño-Acjachema women on reproductive beliefs and practices was conducted 2000 to 2003. This data collection followed several years of work with the southern California American Indian community as a graduate student research assistant, working on the American Indian Health Project then being conducted out of the Center for Health Policy Research at the University of California at Irvine. Laura Williams, M.D., M.P.H., the principal investigator of this project, who is herself Juaneño, was key in introducing me to people in the Juaneño-Acjachema community and in helping me to gain an initial understanding of the community.

Data collection consisted of interviews (in-depth and structured), questionnaires and informal conversations during participant observation at community events. The structured interviews were freelist interviews, in which I asked women several questions about pregnancy and birth practices, eliciting a list of beliefs and reported behaviors for each question. The questions centered on what women should do, or avoid doing, during pregnancy and birth to keep both the child and the mother healthy and free from harm. Freelist interviews were conducted informally with about a dozen women early in the research process.

In-depth interviews were conducted with Juaneño-Acjachema women who had been pregnant and given birth. The interviews focused on the women's experiences during pregnancy and childbirth. Ten women were interviewed, they ranged in age from 40 to 90, with an average age of 63. Five of the women were in their 40s, one in her 50s, two in their 60s, one 75, and one 90. The 90-year-old, interview 19, was interviewed informally at a Juaneño event, with her two adult daughters talking to me with her.

The women averaged 2.5 live births, with the most having had four live births and the fewest having had two live births. They averaged 3.5 pregnancies, with a range of three to five. I asked seven of the women whether they themselves were born at home or in the hospital. Of these, four reported having been born in the hospital, two of these were women in their 40s, one in her 50s, and one 62. Their families at the time of their birth were living in San Juan Capistrano; they had to travel to Orange or Santa Ana for the hospital births. One woman, age 42, reported being born at home in San Juan Capistrano with a midwife attending. The midwife was her relative. Two women reported being born at home with a doctor attending, one in San Juan Capistrano in 1925, and one in El Cajon, San Diego County in 1932. The woman with the doctor attending at her home birth in San Juan Capistrano reports that this was unusual; there had been problems throughout her mother's pregnancy with her, so they knew they would need a doctor. Her brothers were all born at home with a midwife attending.

Most of the women were born in Orange County; one was born in San Diego County, one in Ventura County. Most said they had lived in Orange County for most of their lives. Three reported that they had lived in San Juan Capistrano most of their lives. All were of mixed ethnic background. Their experience with the tribe itself varied. Some had been involved with the tribe their whole lives, some only became directly involved with the tribe as adults.

The vast majority of the women interviewed gave birth in the hospital. One gave birth at home with a nurse-midwife. The women ranged in education level from a High School Diploma or GED to a Master's Degree. Five had a High School Diploma or the equivalent, two had a Master's degree, one is a registered nurse (RN), another a practical nurse (LPN). Age at first pregnancy ranged from 17 to 28 years of age. All the women I asked reported they received prenatal care, although for one woman's pregnancy, it was not until the third trimester.

Following the collection of freelist data, a few of the open-ended interviews, and informal conversations with women from several of the groups; I created a questionnaire that asked about various beliefs and practices regarding pregnancy that had come up in the data already collected. The goal of the questionnaire was to find the degree to which Juaneño-Acjachema women shared beliefs brought up in the open-ended interviews and preliminary freelist interviews.

The questionnaire was administered to thirty-five Juaneño-Acjachema women, all 18 years of age and older. Most women filled out the questionnaire themselves. For elders and a few other women who requested it, I administered the questionnaire. This phase of data collection took place at social and tribal government events of the Juaneño Band of Mission Indians, Acjachema Nation (JBMI). Age of respondents ranged from 19 years to 87 years old. The mean age for the sample was 46.6 years old, with a standard deviation of 16.3 years. One woman did not report her age. The structured interview was not restricted to women who had been pregnant. Of the thirty-five respondents, twenty-six reported having been pregnant. All but eight had children, with one not responding to the question about children. Number of children ranged from one to six for women who have children.

All data collection took place with individuals who self-identified as Juaneño-Acjachema. The Juaneño community has experienced several political splits, with significant animosity and distrust between the groups. Because of this, my data collection was mostly done with a group known as The Juaneño Band of Mission Indians, Acjachema Nation. However, one of the first interviews I did was with someone who later allied with one of the other factions, and I collected data in informal discussions of reproductive health practices with women of a third group, known as the Juaneño Band of Mission Indians.[1] Also, the political factionalization cross-cuts at least some families. While the majority of data collection taking place with one group is a limitation of the study, given that the factionalizations are fairly recent, and that family ties cross-cut the factions, and people periodically shift their allegiances between groups; I do not think that there is significant cultural difference between the groups.[2]

The Juaneño do not have a reservation, or even a particular neighborhood or area where they tend to live. They were brought into the Mission system early on by the Spanish; they had first a small town, and more recently a sprawling suburbia, grow up around where their original village was. It is therefore not surprising to find that most of the women I interviewed had hospital births, and went to a physician for prenatal care during their pregnancies. On the other hand, many women were aware of traditional practices and beliefs. Many women did things they considered to be traditional concurrent with having prenatal medical care and a hospital birth.

The questionnaires showed strong agreement on several biomedical risk factors, showing that these American Indian women were fully cognizant of the risks of, for example, smoking and drinking during pregnancy. This is an important point, as American Indians are generally stereotyped as being problem drinkers, and American Indian women are often thought to be ignorant of the risks of drinking during pregnancy.

---

1. In the Federal Acknowledgement publication, the Juaneño Band of Mission Indians, Acjachema Nation is designated petition 84A and the Juaneño Band of Mission Indians is designated petition 84B. The third group is referred to as an "Interested Party."

2. It must be noted, however, that one of the accusations groups make of each other is that the other group is not legitimately Juaneño-Acjachema. I heard this accusation most often said about the third group, and which is designated by the Bureau of Acknowledgement and Research (BAR) as an "Interested Party" in the Federal Acknowledgement process.

TABLE 4.1 QUESTIONNAIRE ITEMS ON BIOMEDICAL RISK FACTORS

Q: "A pregnant woman should..."	True	False	Don't know	No Answer
Eat right	35 (100%)	0	0	0
Not drink alcohol	35 (100%)	0	0	0
Not use drugs	35 (100%)	0	0	0
Not smoke cigarettes	35 (100%)	0	0	0
Take vitamins	35 (100%)	0	0	0
Go to the doctor's	34 (97.1%)	0	0	1 (2.9%)
Not get X-rays	25 (71.4%)	5 (14.3%)	4 (11.4%)	1 (2.9%)

However, even while the women sought prenatal care and had hospital births, they also had some beliefs and practices that were clearly not mainstream American, and which were clearly different from those of the biomedical model of birth. These practices, the beliefs that they are based on, as well as the ongoing knowledge of these beliefs and practices—even when they are referred to as "old wives' tales"—suggests ongoing cultural difference from mainstream American culture. So that even while one of my informants laments the loss of culture to the Spanish Missionization, there is a culture left. In this chapter, I will explore how that culture is carried on through mother's passing to daughters their advice for how a daughter should manage her pregnancy and birth. This advice is not thought of as "cultural" or "our way" versus another way. It is advice given by a mother to her daughter to ensure the health and welfare of the baby and the daughter. And yet, there are inherent cultural aspects to this. In the biological reproduction, there is social and cultural reproduction: not just that people are reproduced but, *a people*, a society is reproduced.

Many women have little knowledge of pregnancy and birth before they themselves are pregnant. Where do they go for this knowledge? Acjachema women interviewed for this project had two major sources of information during pregnancy: some older woman in her life, most often a mother; and her doctor. Most women spoke a great deal about women in their lives guiding and helping them. These women were sources of both knowledge and support for the new mother during her pregnancy. The woman in Interview 13 brings up her mother immediately in response to the question of what she did to keep healthy during pregnancy:

> I always talked to my Mom. I talked to [husband's] Mom a little bit. Whoever the older ladies in church were at that time. I would talk to them. So it was always older women. It was always older women. [Interview 13]

In passing on health advice to their daughters, women also pass on cultural knowledge. Anthropologists understand birth as socially situated and as part of a culture (Dundes 2003, Kay 1982, Jordan 1980). In the interviews and conversations with Acjachema women, several Acjachemem cultural practices during pregnancy and post-partum arose. Women were educated by their mothers on things to do and not do during pregnancy to keep themselves and their babies healthy and free from harm. Most of the women interviewed gave birth in hospitals and had prenatal care from doctors. However, for most women, birth took place in the home as recently as her mother's generation. These were often managed, as these women reported, by a midwife who was very likely a relative, and might possibly be the one who was called on by others in the community to attend their births.

This was not a case of "cultural mothers versus biomedical doctors" however. One woman, who had endeavored to have a more "traditional" birth, sought the guidance of a spiritual leader of her husband's tribe:[3]

> [W]e sweated in a ceremonial from almost up until the time of birth. So for eight months I sweated and so while I feel our ancestors had a little bit different structure from [my husband's tribe] it was very similar. So we went through the pregnancy with that in mind. There was a ceremonial process of my husband and I walking to gather the sage for the sweat, which was once a week. So I did a little walking that way and of course you know the hot steam is very healthy, you know. [Interview 11]

---

3. She married an American Indian man, although he was not Juaneño. His tribe is being withheld in this writing in an attempt to preserve her anonymity.

However, this same woman was strongly discouraged from a home birth by her Juaneño mother:

> Up until eight months we had a midwife who was in place, and we were going to go that route. But my mother was a nurse, so it was almost a *threat* that I had never experienced from my mother. She was very afraid of me having the baby at home. She didn't want me to have it that way. [Interview 11]

She then finds herself, in the birth process, shifting from the desire to have "natural childbirth" to have some pain relief:

> So we had the baby, and then we said we'll have it at Kaiser, but we won't have any drugs. This was the thing, we were gonna go natural. Well about three hours into the [labor] and all of a sudden all the traditions went out the window and I knew that I needed drugs. Our intentions were, of course, to have this natural. And it is always so humorous to me to have this story that my intentions were very traditional. But I think the sweating was very close to the way the ancestors walked. [Interview 11]

She sought to have a birth that was rooted in her idea—ideas shared by numerous others—of what it is to go through pregnancy and childbirth as an American Indian. How you "do birth" represents who you are as a person.

It was important for her to create an American Indian identity in this and other ways, because she felt that much had been lost:

> Even though we are Juaneño, our traditions are left in the soil of the transition with the Spanish. To say that we had been practicing a lot of our traditional ways for many years isn't really true, because my mother, she was a nurse and worked for hospitals and things like that. Although I did have an aunt that practiced a lot of medicinal plants. And so we did know some of our customs, with the medicines and like that. [Interview 11]

Although she is talking in this quote about her people having lost their traditions, she also notes the use of traditional medicines by her aunt. There was traditional knowledge in her own family that had been carried down since before the Mission period. The force for knowledge shift in her own family seems to be her mother's training as a nurse, and the replacement of traditional medical knowledge with the knowledge of biomedicine. She attempts to carry on traditional practices with the raising of her children. She proudly relates her infant son's positive experience with the sweat:

> And what was very interesting was when I had the baby, a month later we went to a women's sweat for mothers and children. All the mothers had children. We went inside the sweat, and every baby, there were five of them, and my son, so there were about six. And they were crying, miserable. My son, wide-eyed, calm as you can be, was just in there. It was like, this was home to him. He was not upset, because he had been there, because my womb had been there. So that was really incredible. And then we had a special ceremonial sweat for him where all the men who were in the tribe were—and imagine this—you know a sweat is sort of in the shape of an igloo; all the men were in a circle, the burning embers were underneath, and the gourd had the water and they were pouring it on the center stone to make steam. And the spiritual leader who was there, took the water in the gourd, put the water in the mud, mixed up a paste, placed it on my sons feet. And he said, "this little child will walk the path of the red man, he will know his way, and he will always walk the path of his ancestors." [Interview 11]

Following the birth, she and her husband follow what they feel are traditional ways:

> But one thing we did do with the kids was we saved their belly button, fingernail, and some hair, and we made a prayer pouch for them. We put it inside a leather piece and tied it up and kept that for them, and that

was what they were to wear. In the way that—we didn't know if that was really our tradition, but the spiritual leader that married us told us that that was a good medicine for us to make and to keep for the kids. The kids wore them for several years—and then they were gone wherever things go, you know. [Interview 11]

Other things she did with her children as she raised them that she did as part of traditional American Indian culture included breastfeeding until they were two and a half years old, and having her children sleep in the same bed as she and her husband. Here, she talks about using a cradleboard, and the reaction of non-Indian people to her mothering practice:

[The] little one was put in a cradleboard for the first year of his life. The cradleboard is like a baby that is being held at all times. He was absolutely a perfect baby. I mean he never cried, because every time—if he ever fussed I always breastfed him. I breastfed all my kids until they were two-and-a-half. I just really felt that that's the way our ancestors did it. My husband was very supportive in that. *But*, it's the world that didn't like it, and you would get comments. But it didn't matter, because my husband and I, we were in agreement that we were going to do this. So that my oldest one actually nursed the longest and was in the cradleboard the longest, so that's probably the first eight months. But the world didn't like it, and we would go to Denny's or whatever and have the baby in the cradleboard. And I would have people come up to me very rudely and say—it is disgusting what you are doing—because they thought it was abusive to have a child strapped like that. But he never cried. And if he kind of fussed, I would just kind of rock the cradleboard, and he would go to sleep. [Interview 11]

So this woman consciously did things that were traditional American Indian childbirth and child-rearing practices (although clearly not all were Juaneño-Acjachema practices). Yet, she saw a doctor for prenatal care for all of her pregnancies, and each time gave birth in a hospital. This raises two significant points: first, the women in this study are not *either* traditional Juaneño-Acjachemem or culturally American, and second, people do not avoid or reject biomedicine simply because they have cultural health beliefs.

Regarding the second point, the mother of the woman in Interview 11, who insisted that her daughter give birth in a hospital, wanted her daughter to do the traditional post-partum wrapping of herself that will be discussed later in this chapter. So while on the one hand there was the clear influence of biomedicine in the push to have the baby at the hospital, on the other hand, there is the maintenance of cultural practice in the post-partum wrapping. Rejection of a home-birth does not appear to be rejection of the culture in general.

Regarding the first point, there is a tendency to view American Indian culture as only "true" when it matches the culture of 100 years ago. Yet no one would claim that a white American is not American because their culture and use of technology (including medicine) has shifted from that of 100 years ago. The fact that these sorts of claims remain for American Indians is rooted in racism: one is Indian only if one is also "primitive." The correlation is that by being primitive, one is "less." Therefore, one is only considered "Indian" if she can also be considered "less."

Traditional Practices and Beliefs

At this point I will turn to beliefs and practices associated with pregnancy, birth and the post-partum period that were brought up in the interviews, freelists, and conversations with Juaneño-Acjachemem women.

During Pregnancy

A traditional practice that was passed from mother or grandmother to daughter was the belief that if a pregnant woman goes outside while there is an eclipse of the moon occurring, then the child will be born deformed in some way. If she was insistent about going outside (usually to see the moon eclipse itself), then she would be advised to wear metal on her body.

> Everybody wants to go out to see the moon not there, or the passing. She insisted that if I had to go out I had to wear safety pins. She had me like this all across my shirt, and then at the end of my shirt. [Across the] bottom of my shirt. I don't know if there

was any rhyme or reason to it, she just started going through her button jar, pulling out all these pins.

And I wanted to go see, and she said "You can't go out there without this" and I was like "okay-okay." And it was a superstition, I'm sure, but they felt that the moon or the eclipse was going to cause deformities in your child, and she would scare me, tell me the possibilities that could happen. And I said, "Mom, who do you know that actually, that this has happened to, that you base this on?" "I don't know but my Mom said its true, so I'm not taking no chance, that's just how it is." I didn't argue with those things, when she referred to what her mother told her. That was something I wasn't going to argue with. As far as I knew, she knew better than I did. [Interview 12]

In the United States majority society, birth usually takes place in a hospital setting, under the supervision of a doctor or other medical personnel. The anthropologist Bridgette Jordan (1997) has pointed out that the knowledge of the physician has more legitimacy than the knowledge of the woman giving birth. The physician has what Jordan refers to as authoritative knowledge. In the quote above, the woman in Interview 12 acquiesces to the authoritative knowledge of her mother and her grandmother. So here, it is mothers who hold authoritative knowledge regarding birth. Moreover, in Interview 12's mother's generation, the vast majority of women gave birth at home with a midwife, and her mother (Interview 12's grandmother) was one of these midwives, lending more weight to her knowledge in matters of birth and risk. So, if it was a warning that came down from the midwife grandmother, that was something she wasn't going to argue with.

Many women said they didn't know exactly what would happen to their baby if they went out during an eclipse, only that it was dangerous. Some women I spoke with had been told the baby would be born with a birth defect, like a port wine stain, or a cleft palate. The deformities Interview 12's mother noted were both very specific and very serious:

Deformities like no limbs, or it could be if you had twins, the second child, or one of them would be born without a head, or the top of a head. [Interview 12]

As births in more recent generations tend to take place in hospitals, there has been some shift in who holds authoritative knowledge toward the physician, as will be discussed later on in this chapter. However, the traditional beliefs do not disappear entirely with the increased involvement with biomedicine. Later on in Interview 12, I asked her what advice she would give to her own daughter if she were pregnant at some time in the future. Among the things she said was that she would advise her that if there was a lunar eclipse, she should stay indoors, or wear metal if she went outside. Several women I spoke with and interviewed had similar responses: they would (or had) admonish(ed) their daughters to wear metal during an eclipse of the moon "just in case."

As part of the questionnaire I asked women if they believed that going out during an eclipse was dangerous for a pregnant woman. The results appear in Table 4.2.

TABLE 4.2 RESULTS OF QUESTIONNAIRE ITEMS ON MOON ECLIPSE RISK

A pregnant woman should…	True	False	Don't know	No response
Not go out during an eclipse of the moon	9 (25.7)	11 (31.4)	14 (40)	1 (2.9)
When there is an eclipse of the moon, have keys or other metal around her neck or in her pocket so her child won't get a red birth mark	5 (14.3)	15 (42.9)	15 (42.9)	0
If a pregnant woman goes out during an eclipse of the moon, then the baby will be born with a mark	7 (20)	13 (37.1)	10 (28.6)	5 (14.3)

All these questions had a very low percentage of women agreeing that they were true. Just over 25% of the women agreed that it is true that a pregnant woman should not go out during a moon eclipse, while 31.4% said it was false, and 40% said they didn't know. Although the number of women who said this was true is nowhere near a majority, any agreeing at all reveals that there is a belief present that is not present in mainstream American culture. Based on an extensive review of the anthropological literature of reproduction conducted for this project (see Coffman 2004), the discussion of pregnancy and birth with many colleagues, friends, and acquaintances, both as a researcher interested in the topic and as a woman going through childbearing herself as this project was in its formative stages, I suggest that fears of pregnancy risk associated with exposure to a moon eclipse do not appear in mainstream American culture. Thus, even the 40% of women responding that they "don't know" if it is true that it is a risk is significant, as majority culture American women would have very likely simply responded that it is not a risk.[4]

The question about metal to protect the pregnant woman from harm during an eclipse had an even lower agreement rate than the question about avoiding the eclipse generally, with only 14.3% agreeing that it is true. However, this question suffers from poor construction: I not only asked about metal to protect a pregnant woman and her fetus from harm, but I mentioned the specific consequence of a red birthmark. The issue of the use of metal for protection is conflated by the mention of the red birthmark. Women may have answered "not true" or "don't know" because they didn't believe or know that a red birthmark would be the result, even though they might have agreed with the metal-for-protection part.[5] The question: "If a pregnant woman goes out during an eclipse of the moon, then the baby will be born with a mark," specifically asked about a birthmark as a consequence of exposure to a moon eclipse. The low agreement on this item reflects mixed beliefs about the consequence of exposure, as well as the variation in level of agreement about the overall risk of moon-eclipse exposure.

A subset of questionnaires had follow-up questions on traditional Juaneño –Acjachema reproductive practices added, which asked whether women had heard of a particular belief. These were added following several administrations of the questionnaire by me, allowing for comment and discussion by the women I was collecting data from. Many women said that they didn't necessarily believe that it was dangerous for a pregnant woman to go out during the moon eclipse, but that they had

---

4. Of course, this is only suggestive. Such a claim could only be legitimated by actual data collection with American women, i.e. had I given the same questionnaire to a set of white women, the study would have been strengthened in it's claim of a cultural difference.

5. Thus it was a "double-barreled question," asking about two things, making it impossible to sort out which part of it they were responding to. A rookie researcher mistake.

been told it was dangerous by a mother or grandmother. Table 4.3 gives the results of the "heard of" question for avoidance of the lunar eclipse for the subset. Sixty-four percent of the women had heard of this, a much larger percentage than those who responded that they agreed that it was true.

TABLE 4.3 HEARD OF AVOIDANCE OF LUNAR ECLIPSE

	Number	Percent
Yes	9	64
No	4	29

Inquiry with many women, from the interviews to casual conversation, to the administered questionnaire, revealed mixed responses about this belief. As one woman I spoke to put it: "I think it's an old wives' tale." But when pressed whether she would let her daughter go out during an eclipse of the moon while pregnant, she said that she would make her wear metal, just in case. So while "modern" American culture has in many ways overridden prior cultural practice, the beliefs are still there, present in people's minds, even if only as "old wives' tales." Nevertheless, these beliefs differentiate these women from mainstream American culture.

Writing in the 1800s about the Juaneño at and near the Mission, Father Geronimo Boscana documents their reaction to the lunar eclipse:

When they discover any eclipse of the sun or of the moon they start great shouts, cries, and bitter weeping, and this all of them, big and little, throwing dirt into the air, beating on skins, [and] tule mats with great noise. And this they do because they are of the belief that a hideous animal eats the sun or the moon, and they make such exertions in order to scare it away, and they think that if that animal would eat up all the sun or the moon, that is, if it would be a total eclipse, they would all have to die and the world would have to come to an end. I believe at the time of the eclipse when they make such a noise, they are making a supplication to the God Chinigchinix, because I saw (at one which there was in the year 1813 and at another in 1822), of the sun, that when the eclipse was over the old men began their dance like giving him thanks for having delivered him from that animal. [Harrington 1934]

He does not specifically mention pregnant women. This is not surprising, though, as there might not have been any in his vicinity during the witnessing of the event (perhaps they were all obedient to their mothers and remained indoors). Or he may have simply not attended to women in particular.

The anthropologist Alfred Kroeber, who extensively studied American Indians, wrote the following about California Indians:

> When a new moon shows itself they make a great outcry, which manifests their interest...If there is an eclipse of the sun or of the moon, they shout with still louder outcries, beating the ground, skins, or mats with sticks, which shows their concern or uneasiness. (Kroeber 1976: 11)

Kelly (1965) relates a similar practice regarding pregnancy among people in the Laguna area of Northern Mexico. She says that there is a

> local manifestation of an Ancient Mexican belief that if a pregnant woman views an eclipse she may abort or her baby may be born with a harelip or other malformation. These same beliefs are widespread in Mexico today. (Kelly 1965:9)

The woman avoided this harm by the carrying of an obsidian blade. Kelly relates that her current informants have modified this practice: "[the pregnant woman] places a key, or some other iron object, such as scissors, at her waist" (1965:9). If she is does not do this the child will be born deformed because "the moon will eat a piece of the lip or the hand" and that those who are clubfooted have also been harmed by an eclipse (Kelly 1965:9). Kelly notes that the belief in the damage to the fetus by the eclipse is most likely "ancient native Mexican," suggesting it is of indigenous origin and not a Spanish import (1965:116).

Beliefs that eclipses are a dangerous time range far and wide historically and cross culturally. In India, for example, the eclipse of the sun is viewed as dangerous. During an eclipse one may not eat or cook, and any food cooked before the eclipse should not be consumed but should be thrown out. Additionally, it is believed that a woman who is pregnant should not sew during an eclipse of the sun, doing so will cause her child to be born with a deformity (Thaindian News 2010). This is an interesting similarity to the Juaneño restriction on women who are pregnant, although it is for a sun eclipse rather than a moon eclipse.

In ancient China, the people believed that a dragon was eating the moon or sun during an eclipse (Harley 1885). This belief was shared by pre-modern peoples from Europe to Asia to Africa (Harley 1885). Many peoples believe that the eclipse of the moon is a bad omen, a portent of crop failure, disaster, or illness (Milan 2000, Harley 1885).

The eclipse, whether it is of the sun or moon, is a phenomenon which historically and cross-culturally caused fear, and provoked behaviors to control that fear. The question is: why the fear? Perhaps this is obvious: the loss of light, the obscuring of the sun or moon. However, eclipses, although infrequent, are not unheard of phenomena. They do not in reality bring any harm. So why the level of taboo associated with them, and why, specifically, the taboos on pregnant women?

Pregnancy and birth are a period of transition and of risk for the woman and for those socially connected to her. Van Gennep, in 1908, documented that pregnancy is treated as a time of transition, or liminality (see also Turner 1969). The pregnant woman is in a state of "betwixt and between" and in a way is outside of society, in a state of difference, a state of flux. This state requires ritual to protect the woman and to protect the society from the overflow of this liminal state into the society as a whole.

Turner, building on the work of Van Gennep in his discussion of liminality and transition and its management by ritual, likens this state to that of an eclipse:

> Thus, liminality is frequently likened to death, *to being in the womb*, to invisibility, to darkness, to bisexuality, to the wilderness, and *to an eclipse of the sun or moon*. (Turner 1969: 95, italics mine)

Pregnancy is liminal. The moon eclipse is liminal. Liminality is a risky state. Perhaps combined, the two states of liminality, the event of an eclipse, and a woman's state of being pregnant, are overwhelming in their risk, suggesting serious danger to a woman's unborn child.

Diet During Pregnancy

Some women spoke of a special post-partum diet, which will be discussed later in this chapter. Most of the discussion about diet during pregnancy entailed use of phrases like "eat right" or "watch your diet" with little elaboration on exactly what they meant. Many women said that they were admonished by their mothers to "eat well" and to drink plenty of water. The questionnaire included a question that women should "eat right" during pregnancy. This item was followed by the open-ended question: "What should she eat?" Three of the women left the question unanswered, summary responses from the rest appear in table 4.4. The most-listed specific items, were vegetables (22 occurrences), fruit (9), meat (9, 11 if fish is included), and dairy (7). Many of the women didn't mention specific food items but gave general statements like "balanced" (12 occurrences), and, less frequently "don't over eat," eat when hungry," "enough for two," etc. The general question about eating right had a high level of agreement, with 100% of the women agreeing that a pregnant woman should eat right.[6]

---

6. Of course, this is the kind of question that it would be unlikely to get disagreement with. The follow-up question asking for specifics was the greater purpose of the item's inclusion in the questionnaire.

TABLE 4.4 EAT RIGHT RESPONSES

Word or phrase	Occurrences
Vegetables (including specific vegetable named)	22
Balanced, four food groups, all the basics	12
Fruit (including specific fruit named)	9
Meat, red meat, chicken	9
Dairy	7
Healthy	4
Drink lots of fluids/drink plenty of water	4
Calcium	3
Protein	3
Nonfat/low-fat	2
Vitamins/prenatal vitamins	2
Rice	2
Beans	2
Don't over eat; not more than usual	2
Nourishing food, nourishment for the baby	2
Fish	2
Eat when hungry	1
Soy	1
No salt	1
Enough for two	1
Not junk food	1
Don't go a long time without eating	1
Oatmeal	1
Clean	1
Atole*	1
Food with iron	1
Potassium	1
Bread	1
Anything else she craves	1

* A mixture of flour paste, milk, and sugar. Bring to a boil. It is a drink given also to children when they are sick.

Activity Level

Walking and keeping to one's previous activity level were often mentioned by women. These were specific admonitions by women's mothers:

> I kept all my regular activities, though. My Mom always said all the housekeeping and stuff you do is good exercise, so keep doing what you do. You should have common sense to know what's overdoing it. You can't kill yourself, so if you're tired, just rest. [Interview 13]

Interview 12 was admonished to walk:

> But the moment I knew, the night that I knew I conceived, I knew I had a change in my life. Nobody believed me but my Mom. I was only 17, but I just knew that there was something different that was happening to me. From that point on I just—what she made me do was *walk every day.* Every day. Because I lived at home with her until I got married. And so I did. And it wasn't a matter of how long I walked— even if it was a matter of just down to the end of the street and back. And she swore that would be easier on my birth, to have strong muscles on my stomach and lower back. I had to listen to her, I mean a woman having twelve children, she must have known something.

Use of Herbs

Several of the women reported using plants gathered in the local area in the treatment of pregnancy-related discomforts. Interview 12, again, under the direction of her mother:

> I basically followed my mother's direction as far as during the pregnancy what I was feeling. If I had cramps, any kind of, well it would feel like contractions, a little pulling down underneath there, right where your stomach [is]. And I used to get headaches. She would put this plant, she would take this plant

and boil it in water, I believe it was Yerba Buena. But it was tea that she made me drink [groaning in distaste]. [Interview 12]

This same plant, Yerba Buena, is also mentioned specifically by another woman:

Yerba Buena in Spanish. It's like that mint. It means good weed. It's like mint tea, you get it and boil it. It's good for the morning sickness. It does help. Even now when I have an upset stomach. . . It's even better if you grow some. I used to have some right outside the house. [Interview 13]

The plant, Yerba Buena, is a California native, *Micromeria chamissonis*, classified in the division Magnoliophyta, class Magnoliopsida, order Lamiales, family Labiatae (Columbia Encyclopedia 2003). It is sometimes referred to as "Marsh Mint" and is related to mint. Other women reported specifically being given mint; it is unclear whether this was mint or Yerba Buena. The woman in Interview 11 notes the use that mint as well as white sage, which is used by many Native Americans for smudging:

I did use the mint when I was sick, and then we gave the kids that, too. And then the sage. We actually kind of stewed it, and took that. [Interview 11]

Other plants were also mentioned, and for uses other than teas:

I remember my feet would swell... She [her mother] would put my feet in a pail of cool water, and I don't know what she would put in it, I know it wasn't Epsom salt, but it was something more of a plant. It had a scent. And I can't remember if it was a mint scent, I can't recall the plant. It was just like, normal, and you didn't question what. And I'm sorry I didn't, I'm sorry I didn't ask why. [Interview 12]

Interviewee 11 above mentions stewing sage for a tea. Sage is used today among the Juaneño in ceremony. It is burned and people are smudged with it, which simply means that you allow the smoke to flow over them. It grows locally and people often collect it while hiking—or hike for the purpose of collecting it.

Bathing During Pregnancy

A very small number of women mentioned restrictions on bathing, as in being submerged in water, during pregnancy.

> Couldn't take no hot baths, and that's all we had in our home was a bathtub, we didn't have a shower, so I had to—basically was on my knees washing myself with soap and hot water. [Interview 12]

This woman didn't know the reason behind not taking a hot bath. In a discussion with a group of women from the Juaneño Band of Mission Indians faction, several of the women agreed that one should not take a bath for forty days before or after the birth, and also not while you are menstruating. The women said that this is "because you are open." The issue was submergence of the entire body, allowing water to enter the neck of the uterus (in this belief set).

In the questionnaire, the question that asked about the avoidance of bathing before and after the birth was disagreed with by 62.9% of the respondents. Twenty-five percent agreed that a woman should avoid bathing before and after the birth, and 11.4% responded that they didn't know.

Birthing

The vast majority of Juaneño-Acjachemem women I spoke with gave birth in the hospital. Only one woman gave birth with a midwife at home, and this was not a Juaneño woman as midwife, like people reported their mothers and grandmothers had, but a medically trained nurse-midwife. Another woman, as discussed in the opening of this chapter, had sought to "be traditional" and give birth at home with a midwife, but ended up having a hospital birth due to her mother's fear of a home birth. I opened every interview with a question about how childbirth was for the interviewees' mother, which elicited stories of birthing a generation previous to these women. At that time, almost all the births took place at home with a midwife. These home birth experiences will be discussed first, followed by the hospital births.

Home Births

Interview 17 was 69 years old at the time of the interview. When asked what her mother did for childbirth, she gave the following account of birthing in the 1930s:

> My grandmother was the one that was more in charge of what women should do in preparation for the birth. So my mother was wrapped in pieces of material that had been washed and well rinsed. And they were put in the oven, so that they would be sort of sterilized. They were put in the wood stove oven. So the part top was kind of burnt, but the inside was clean. And she would prepare with olive oil.
>
> They would have olive oil on hand, and the sterilized cloth, which wasn't really sterile, but it was clean. And had a board to put under the mother so that when the baby came, the mattress or the underneath would not be cradled, but would hold the back so it was flat.
>
> It would be a little difficult if your bottom is sunk and the baby was coming. And look, what did we have in those days? You were lucky if you had a mattress and that was homemade, so there was a cradle, what would you call it, depression or a dip?....so it would keep the back, the spine and the buttocks straight so when the baby would come it would, come out. [Interview 17]

For the Juaneño-Acjachema the traditional midwife was a creature of necessity. Prior to the 1950s, medical care was not readily accessible to the people of San Juan Capistrano and the other rural areas of southern California. Other rural peoples shared such conditions during this time period (cf Fraser 1995). The traditional midwife was a community member, often a relative, who helped during births and other minor health problems. Such midwives were always females. Women did not make a conscious choice in these settings to use a midwife: she was the only choice. The exception being the few cases where it was known that there would or could be serious problems, in which case the woman would make the trip up to Anaheim or wherever the nearest hospital was.

Hospital Births

Many women gave birth in the hospital setting. In the birthing setting, as in any domain, there are various knowledge systems possible. One knowledge system often comes to dominate the situation, usually through its association with those in power, and also via its efficacy in that particular domain (Jordan 1997). In the United States, biomedicine is the knowledge system that has authority in the domain of birth and pregnancy (Clark and Olesen 1999, Davis-Floyd 1992, Jordan 1980, 1997, Mitford 1992). This is the system that is viewed as correct and legitimate. Those who believe other things are characterized as "backward, ignorant, naïve, or troublemakers" (Jordan 1997: 57). Jordan (1997) for example, details how in the process of a birth, the woman's need to push and thus complete the birth is ignored. She is told that she cannot push until the doctor pronounces her ready to push through a physical examination and through an examination of the technological information gathered via the fetal monitor. His knowledge counts, hers does not.

Some of the women I interviewed had directly experienced the discounting of their knowledge, and even their experience of their own body, by the medical system that gave more authority to the doctor and to technology.

The women in Interview 12, in her third pregnancy, perceived herself to be in labor. She was having contractions, cramping, and was spotting blood. Her husband was traveling, so she brought her children to a relative's house and drove herself the thirty miles to the hospital. She was sent home that evening, drove back at three in the morning, and was again sent home, both times because her cervix was not dilated enough.

> And about three in the morning, I drove myself back, they sent me home, they said I was just barely three-and-a-half. But I was really hurting by then. I couldn't stand. I couldn't sit. I couldn't walk. I was

hurting, I was crying. I was bleeding. My doctor had come in—it was only the emergency room nurse who had seen me before—and said, "oh you're only [dilated] so much." [Interview 12]

She was finally admitted the third time, but only after she told her doctor that her husband was out of town for several days and that she had been driving herself back and forth.

This woman's bodily experience—that she was having contractions, that she was bleeding—was discounted. The only thing that counted were the technological measurements of her cervix, and the doctor's evaluation of them. This woman herself lent credence to this framework: it was "only the nurse," she said, who saw her the first time. Her doctor would better ascertain her true state: that she was in fact in labor. But he, relying on the measurement of her cervix, said that she was not and sent her home again. It is only through appealing to the fact of the absence of her husband to drive her that she was finally admitted.

Another woman I interviewed also found her bodily experience, and her own knowledge of what was going on in her body, was discounted in favor of a technological test.

What happened that morning is kind of funny 'cause I woke him [husband] up, my water broke in the bed. 'cause you know it's your first time you're not sure. And I said it must be because I couldn't go to the bathroom this much. And how it is with health services these days, you have to go here, you have to go there. Well they sent us up to the Long Beach location. And they did check me out there. And then I remember too the girl, they put that paper, to do the litmus test. And the girl says "are you sure your water broke?'" I said, "Lookit, as far as I know, that's what it is." And she did it again, "Well, I guess so, but you know you're gonna have to—" And they sent us down to Palm Hospital in Garden Grove. And so I had just started contractions. [Interview 13]

So her belief that her water broke is challenged by the litmus test. A woman's experience of her own body is deemed less important than the technology. The authoritative knowledge is not hers, but the hospital staff's. She is finally able to convince the staff person she sees that her water did break.

Interview 14 was the one woman who had home births for all her children. However, these also took place within a biomedical context, with the authoritative knowledge being that linked to biomedicine. She had experience with both nurse-midwives and lay-midwives, but both had linkages to hospitals and doctors to back them up. They relied on measures of cervical dilation, and strict timings of when contractions should be coming (2 minutes apart) before calling the midwives to come. Also, for her first birth, which was with a nurse-midwife, it was required that a doctor be present for the actual birth. So although this is a home-birth and a birth with a midwife, it is very different from the kind of midwifery that women of the previous generation experienced.

Post-Partum Care

> The…custom of these Indians…was that at every childbirth, from the time the woman brought forth, the husband had to go on a diet like the woman herself, and this consists mainly in his not being able to leave the house except to bring wood and water, [and] in not eating meat or fish or other foods forbidden to them. This diet usually lasted some 15 days…and now that they are Christian they still observe it, for they are of belief that if they …do not observe this diet…the baby will die. (Harrington 1934:26)

As Boscana observed for the Juaneño-Acjachema in the Mission San Juan Capistrano in the 1800s, the time shortly after the birth of a child is a time in which care must be taken to preserve the health and welfare of the child, and that the behavior of the parents has a direct affect on this.

Many of the women I interviewed reported receiving help from mothers or other older women following the birth. Here we see the continuation of the mothers' passing on of traditional knowledge and practice. Such practices included post-partum wrapping of the woman, and a forty-day post-partum period in which there are restrictions on diet and certain activities. Interview 15, who was 76 years old at the time of the interview, talks about the time following birth as a time in which the woman was vulnerable:

> She [her mother] said for me to take care of myself. Because after a birth it is easy to get sick or bleed or something like that. And she said I wasn't to go outside and get cold and all that stuff. We had to stay indoors forty days. Of course we didn't do that all the time, behind my mother's back we'd go out. [And] we had to go to the bathroom outside at the time. We had an outhouse. [Interview 15]

She also reports that she went and stayed with her mother following her hospital birth:

> After the birth in the hospital I stayed for fifteen days. Then I came home. Of course I went to my mother's. I didn't go directly home. I stayed with her almost, about a week and a half, not quite two weeks. [Interview 15]

Another woman reports that it was her grandmother who came to help her, and that she followed traditional practices with her grandmother's guidance, even though she had her baby in the hospital:

> I had my children in the hospital….my grandmother flew down … to be there when I had my daughter and to wrap me and to be with me for a few days, and then I knew what to do. [Interview 17]

Another woman talks about her mother being there and helping out, this one with the healing of her stitches following an episiotomy:

> But I had a lot of stitches. So my mother was there, after I got home from the hospital, and she had heat lamps. So about an hour every day under a heat lamp. To dry the stitches. [Interview 18]

So the presence of their mother was important for these women following the birth, and it was the mother who taught the cultural practices like wrapping, as well as less cultural, but nevertheless important help like with the housework, or caring for older children while the woman recovered.

In Interview 17, the woman mentions the need to rest, though she does not say specifically that one had to stay in the house for forty days. She then goes into some more detail in explaining that a woman could not bathe in a shower or bath, but could have a sponge bath:

> It was customary, yes. That after a birth you rested, and kept a diet for forty days. You did not bathe—oh that was horrible—you did not bathe. ....a sponge bath [was okay]. But not any showers or baths. No sex. [Interview 17]

This woman was not the only one to mention no sex for forty days:

> You were talking about—the things that my mother did. She did say to refrain from after a baby was born. Things that I learned from my mother or from the women in my family, they said to refrain from sex for at least forty days. [Interview 14]

The specifics of the diet were explained by Interviewee 17:

> No tomatoes. No acid, or lemons or grapefruit or anything acidy. Orange juice, nothing like that. It was all herbal tea. We had a lot of peppermint tea, cinnamon tea, chamomile—which is very healing. Lots of chamomile. No ice, nothing cold. [Interview 17]

When asked why there were these restrictions, this woman said that she did not know why they were there or what would happen if you broke them.

In a discussion I had with a group of Juaneño-Acjachemem women from the Juaneño Band of Mission Indians (84B) faction, similar restrictions came up for women when they were menstruating. The women in this group mentioned nothing acidic. Lemons, tomatoes and plums were specifically mentioned by these women as foods to avoid. One should not bathe while menstruating; one should not wash their hair while menstruating. These women also said that a menstruating woman should not walk barefoot in a creek.

When asked why these restrictions were there and what would happen if women broke them, the women responded that these restrictions are there "because you are open" and "if you do these things you will get arthritis or other sickness when you are older." These women also said, like the woman above said her grandmother told her, that salty or acidic foods would cause worse cramps.

Kroeber (1971a), discussing Southern California Indians generally, notes rites of passage following a girl's first menses, and that, "direct physiological treatment [of the girl] is needed to ensure future health" (Kroeber 1971a: 50). This includes the maintenance of warmth, so the girl must not drink cold water and must bathe only in heated water. Kroeber also notes that for what he calls the "region of Gabrieleño-Luiseño influence," which presumably includes the Acjachema, as they were geographically situated between the two groups, "the girl is cooked or roasted, as it were, in a pit" (1971: 50). Boscana describes this "roasting" for the Juaneño: On a woman's "arrival on womanhood" (menarche) a hole was made in the ground "in shape resembling a grave" and about two feet deep (Harrington 1934:47). The hole was filled with stones and burning coals, the coals were removed when the stones were heated. Branches of California mugwort, sedge or sumac, were laid on the hole to make a bed, the bed was decorated with beads and feathers, and the young woman laid on it, eating and drinking little, for three days. Older women with painted faces sang over her; younger women danced (Harrington 1934:47).

Kroeber (1971a) further notes that for the Luiseños, there were trials of running for the girl, she used a head scratcher, so as not to touch her head with her hands, fasts from meat and salt, and there was a tobacco-eating ordeal. This is also the time when she receives her facial tattoos, which were straight lines on her chin and cheeks radiating out from her lower lip. There was the creation of a sand painting, and rock paintings. During my fieldwork I was taken to a site in the local Cleveland National Forest lands that was said to be one of the places where these rites were performed. There were seven-foot high boulders, situated next to a stream, which had the holes on top that were used for grinding acorns, and that had, on the side adjacent to the creek, ancient rock paintings, which were simple line drawings of what appeared to be a sun and moon and line figures of people.

Postpartum Wrapping of the Woman

A number of women talked about being wrapped following birth. The women who did this had a mother or grandmother present or around after the birth. The purpose of the wrapping seems to have been to get the woman's body back into shape after pregnancy and birth, as is told by this 69-year-old Juaneño-Acjachema woman:

> Well, after birth we would be wrapped. We would be wrapped with the muslin from here all the way wrapped to here [indicates from lower belly to just under breasts]. To keep everything warm and help with the swelling and the process of [the swelling] going down after you have the baby. And my gosh, after I had my children I was just like I didn't have any. I was so slender. And my mother kept a very good shape. Fourteen children and she had a good body. [Interview 17]

This woman notes that you keep the wrap on for thirty days, close to the same time period as the diet and behavioral restrictions.

> Through maybe, I'd say, thirty days. The wrap is changed. It's taken off and wrapped, and checked to see how we were doing. And my grandmother knew if we were in place or not. [Interview 17]

For this woman, her mother was actively involved in the wrapping:

> I think when I got home from the hospital, the first thing she did was she got some baby receiving blankets I had gotten. She put two together and pinned them both so it was long enough to go around my stomach and she pinned them right here [indicates sides along waist] on the side here. And she bound me up. And you know, you're cramping and [groans] after you had a baby, But she was—she said "this is going to be bet-

ter for you, its going to hold your tummy, yeah you're going to be cramping, but this will be better for you, it pushes your uterus in." "Okay, Mom." [Interview 12]

A few of the women said that they knew about wrapping, but didn't do it. Interview 18 said that her grandmother suggested that she wrap, but that she chose not to. Surprisingly, the woman in Interview 11, who had gone to great lengths to be traditional in her birth preparations, consulting a traditional healer from her husband's tribe and participating in sweat lodge ceremonies before and after the birth, declined her mother's advice to wrap post-partum.

Interview 17, in discussing her daughter, said that her daughter didn't wrap post-partum, but wore a girdle, and that she tried to follow the forty-day restriction on diet and bathing. Her husband, who was white, was resistant and not supporting. According to the woman in Interview 17, her daughter was able to maintain the dietary, sexual, and bathing restrictions for about thirty days, even in the face of lack of support from her husband. She did do the post-partum restrictions for about thirty days though.

This chapter has examined cultural beliefs and practices regarding pregnancy and birth among Juaneño-Acjachema women. The women in this group clearly have some differences from mainstream American culture. Even if these beliefs are now sometimes only referred to as superstitions or old wives' tales, they still serve to differentiate this group. This chapter has also demonstrated the importance of mothers in educating their daughters about childbearing, and how this serves to not only contribute to the reproduction of biological people, but also is the reproduction of a culture. This suggests that with the shift toward medicalized hospital births that was eventually accomplished in the United States as a whole (rural areas like San Juan Capistrano having remained isolated and using midwives up through the 1950s) not only took control of birthing away from women (as is frequently lamented by anthropologists) but also contributed to culture loss for sub-cultural groups in the United States.

As the authority of the biomedical model became pervasive, and as pregnancy and birth became something that is managed by and takes place in medical institutions, rather than in home settings and managed primarily by family members; traditional Juaneño knowledge regarding birth and pregnancy came to be superseded by the biomedical model.

Nevertheless, the idea that they, as Juaneño-Acjachema, do things differently than whites or Hispanics is still present. This exists in their personal identity practices, as discussed in the chapter preceding this one, as well as in overt attempts to be traditional in their birth and birth preparations, as with the woman who participated in sweatlodge ceremonies to prepare for childbirth.

chapter 5

Conclusion

The previous chapters have laid out the history of the Juaneño-Acjachema people, how they came to be conquered and enslaved by the Spanish, and how they struggle to maintain their identity as Juaneño today. This chapter takes a closer look at the current state of their petition for Federal Acknowledgement.

On March 11, 2011 the Bureau of Indian Affairs announced that it had issued a Final Determination (FD) on the two Juaneño groups' petitions for federal acknowledgement. Both the Juaneño Band of Mission Indians, Acjachema Nation (petition 84A) and the Juaneño Band of Mission Indians (petition 84B) were denied acknowledgement as a tribe to whom the federal government has ongoing treaty obligations. This has (almost) brought to a conclusion a process begun in 1982 with the Juaneño's first submission of a Letter of Intent to Petition for Federal Acknowledgement, a nineteen-years-long process (see table 5.1).

TABLE 5.1 TIMELINE FOR PETITION FOR FEDERAL
ACKNOWLEDGEMENT BY THE JUANEÑO[1]

1982	Submitted letter of intent to petition ("JBM" group).
1988	Submitted initial materials to petition.
1990	Technical Assistance Review/Obvious Deficiency letter sent.
1993	Additional materials submitted by JBM. JBM requests to be placed on the "Ready, Waiting for Active Consideration" list. Placed on Ready List.
1994	Disputed election in the JBM.
1995	Juaneño's petition removed from Ready List, pending revision of their membership rolls following factioning of the tribe after disputed election.
1996	Placed on Ready List again. Second group, formed following disputed election, submits petition. Group calls itself The Juaneño Band of Mission Indians (JBB by OFA), designated Petition 84b, the first group, the Juaneño Band of Mission Indians, Acjachema Nation (JBMI) is designated Petition 84a, OFA refers to them as "JBA"
1998, 1999, 2000	JBMI (84a) submits additional documents.
2005	JBMI (84a) submits new set of petition materials. JBB (84b) submits letter of request the two groups be considered simultaneously. Both groups go on Active Consideration.
2007	Proposed Finding Against Federal Acknowledgement issued. JBMI and JBB submit responses within the 90-day response period.
2011	Final Determination Against Federal Acknowledgement issued.

(Bureau of Indian Affairs 2007a, 2007b)

1. Documents related to the petitions appear on the BIA website at: http://www.bia.gov/WhoWeAre/AS-IA/OFA/ADCList/ActivePetitions.htm.

Many criticize the process of petitioning for Federal Acknowledgement as both taking too long and as having criteria which are too stringent. According to the National Congress of American Indians:

> Each of the criteria demands exceptional anthropological, historical, and genealogical research and presentation of evidence. The vast majority of petitioners do not meet these strict standards, and far more petitions have been denied than accepted. In fact, only about 8% of the total number of petitioning tribes have been individually recognized since 1960. (NCAI 2011)

"Federal Acknowledgement" means that the United States government formally acknowledges ongoing treaty obligations to an American Indian tribe. During the process of invasion and conquest of what would become the U.S., Europeans made treaties and agreements with the indigenous people already living there. Some of these were land-purchase agreements, some of these were treaties to end a military conflict. As discussed in Chapter 3, indigenous peoples of the Americas were treated as sovereign nations by the colonies and then by the early U.S. government. This sovereign status has been upheld by U.S. law and legal rulings. Today, the U.S. government continues to honor some of the promises made in the historical treaties, and to honor the idea of "owing something" to American Indians. Who exactly is owed to is determined through federal acknowledgement.

Federal acknowledgement allows tribes access to federal funds for health, education and social service programs, and they are given federal money to purchase land in their indigenous area, which will be held in trust for them by the federal government. Many tribes can run casinos, as per the laws reviewed in Chapter 3 of this book. The fact that they can run casinos has led to the politicization of the federal acknowledgement process. Many groups which should not have any say whatsoever in the process consider themselves to have a say. For example, following the issuance of the Proposed Finding for the Juaneño there was a comment period in which interested parties could submit comments. One of the groups to submit comment on the federal acknowledgement of the Juaneño was a group calling itself "California Cities for Self Reliance." As noted in the Final Determination for Petition 84A:

An interested party, the "California Cities for Self Reliance, Joint Powers Authority" (JPA), submitted, as comment on the JBA and JBB PFs [Proposed Findings], a 69-page document written by James P. Lynch (the Lynch Report) (JPA 5/9/2008). [BIA 2011a: 5]

This organization is a consortium of gambling organizations (card rooms) in Los Angeles County. Although the front page of their website attempts to portray the group as somehow representing cities and people in Los Angeles, their "About" page reveals their true identity:

> California Cities for Self Reliance, a joint powers authority, was established in July 2001. Its members include the cities of Bell Gardens, Commerce, Compton, Gardena, Hawaiian Gardens, and Inglewood...
>
> The purpose of California Cities for Self Reliance is to promote and protect the card club gaming economy of the state of California and its member cities in order to enhance the economic climate and improve the quality of life for the residents in the Southern California region.
>
> [California Cities for Self Reliance 2011]

Their "interest" in the Federal Acknowledgement of the Juaneño-Acjachema is the possibility that if the Juaneño received federal acknowledgement, they might eventually be able to open a casino, which would compete with their card rooms. It is unclear why the BIA gave any consideration at all to the submission of comments by an organization that not only has such a clear-cut economic interest in preventing the Juaneños from gaining Federal Acknowledgement, but is based in a different county in southern California. The cities they represent are all at least an hour's drive from San Juan Capistrano, and none of them are encompassed in the traditional indigenous territories of the Juaneño-Acjachema.

Federal Acknowledgement was formalized in 1978 with the issuance of CFR 25 83, in order to bring consistency to the process. Prior to this, tribes were recognized as tribes to whom the federal government had ongoing obligations in various ways, including decisions by the Assistant Secretary of the Interior, the Deputy Commissioner for Indian

Affairs, and acknowledgement by Congressional Act (GAO 2001). According to a federal report evaluating the federal acknowledgement process, the "essential prerequisite" for federal acknowledgement is "the tribe's continuous existence as a political entity since a time when the federal government broadly acknowledged a political relationship with all Indian tribes," (GAO 2001:24). CFR 25 83 also establishes that a group must demonstrate social existence, including that they are separate from the rest of the society.

However, the process is flawed in several ways. It takes much longer than the federal government originally anticipated to resolve petitions: the anticipated resolution time was two years; the actual average resolution time, at the time of the GAO report, was fifteen years (GAO 2001). The Juaneño-Acjachema submitted their petition in 1988; they did not receive a final determination until 2011, this time frame is not unusual. The GAO report pointed out that the subdivision of the BIA that deals with petitions, the Office of Federal Acknowledgement (OFA), is seriously understaffed. The report also stated that there are not specific timelines for completion of many stages of the process, leading to what they refer to as a lack of urgency on the part of OFA to complete petitions (GAO 2001). For some steps in the process, the OFA does have specific deadlines for completion. However, I noted that in the Juaneño petition, OFA granted itself extensions to these deadlines multiple times.

Another major flaw in the federal acknowledgement process is the lack of clarity in the criteria itself. The GAO report "Improvements Needed in Tribal Acknowledgement Process" states:

> Because of weaknesses in the acknowledgement process, the basis for BIA's tribal acknowledgement decisions is not always clear and the length of time involved can be substantial. First, while there are set criteria that petitioners must meet to be granted acknowledgement, there is no clear guidance that explains how to interpret key aspects of the criteria. For example, it is not always clear what level of evidence is sufficient to demonstrate a tribe's continuous existence over a period of time—one of the key aspects of the criteria. As a result, there is less certainty about the basis of acknowledgement decisions. (Government Accountability Office 2001: 2-3)

The Office of Federal Acknowledgement gives examples of what might be documentation, but there is a lack of clarity and of clarification. The JBMI (petition 84a) specifically requested more information and clarification, and were told to simply see the information that was already available. The Office of Federal Acknowledgement provides "technical assistance" to tribes that are petitioning. The following is an excerpt from a technical assistance letter written by the OFA to the JBMI, as a follow up to a phone conference. During the phone conference, the JBMI posed a question regarding historical evidence, which the OFA responds to:

> [Question from JBMI] Due to the fact that California has a history of dealing with tribes differently than other parts of the United States, what primary historical documents are required or not required by the OFA during the period of 1850 to the present?

> [OFA Response]
> The regulations do not specify what types of primary historical documents a petitioner is required to submit. Under criterion 83.7(a), the regulations list some types of evidence that may be relied upon in demonstrating external identification of the group since 1900 (see 83.7(a)(1)(6)). For criteria 83.7(b) and (c), the regulations state that the existence of community and political influence shall be demonstrated on a substantially continuous basis from first sustained contact with non-Indians throughout the group's history to the present. The petitioner is encouraged to review the regulations under 83.7(b)(I) and (2) and 83.7(c) (I) and (2) for further details on the combinations of various types of evidence that might show community and political influence. Criterion 83.7(e) requires that the petitioner's membership consists of individuals who descend from a historical tribe or tribes which combined and functioned as an autonomous single political entity. The petitioner should review the types of evidence acceptable to the Secretary, which can be used for this purpose (83.7(e)(l)). During the infor-

mal technical assistance review, OFA researchers also described other records that might be useful evidence such as mission election records, mission baptismal, marriage and burial records and certificates, local records, and Federal and state censuses. (OFA 2005:2)

The JBMI specifically asked for more information and more clarification, and the OFA response was to direct them to information that the tribe already had. So the criteria remain fairly vague. See Appendix 2 for the full text of CFR 25 83.7, which lists all the types of evidence that are acceptable.

Another weakness of process pointed out by the GAO report is a lack of clarity as to how long a gap in documentation of existence is allowable:

Concerns over what constitutes continuous existence have centered on the allowable gap in time during which there is limited or no evidence that a petitioner has met one or more of these criteria. In one case, the technical staff recommended that a petitioner not be recognized because there was a 70-year period for which there was no evidence that the petitioner satisfied the criteria for continuous existence as a distinct community exhibiting political authority. The technical staff concluded that a 70-year evidentiary gap was too long to support a finding of continuous existence. *The staff based its conclusion on precedent established through previous decisions where the absence of evidence for shorter periods of time had served as grounds for finding that petitioners did not meet these criteria.* However, in this case, the Assistant Secretary issued a proposed finding to recognize the petitioner, concluding that continuous existence could be presumed despite the lack of specific evidence for a 70-year period. (GAO 2001: 12, emphasis mine).

This lack of specificity allows for inconsistencies in the process, other tribes had been refused Federal Acknowledgement on the basis of having a gap on documentation that is less that 70 years, this one gets acknowledgement even with a gap of 70 years. As we will see below, one of the reasons given for not granting the JBMI Federal Acknowledgement was a supposed gap of 97 years in documentation (1900-1997). It is unclear why 97 years is too long a time, while 70 years is not. Moreover, the JBMI submitted documentation of their existence for that time period. The OFA staff rejected this documentation as insufficient for demonstrating their existence. This is problematic given their lack of true clarification of what would be sufficient or viable evidence. This will be further discussed later in this chapter.

Another area that the GAO found inconsistency and a lack of clarity was with the percent of a group that must have genealogically documented descent from the historical tribe:

> Another key aspect of criteria that has stirred up controversy and created uncertainty is the proportion of a petitioner's membership that must demonstrate that it meets the criterion of descent from a historic Indian tribe. In one case, the technical staff recommended that a petitioner not be recognized because the petitioner could only demonstrate that 48% of its members were descendents. The technical staff concluded that finding that the petitioner had satisfied this criterion would have been a departure from precedent established through previous decisions in which petitioners found to meet this criterion had demonstrated a higher percentage of membership descent from a historic tribe. *However, in the proposed finding, the Assistant Secretary found that the petitioner satisfied the criterion.* The Assistant Secretary told us that this decision was not consistent with previous decisions by other Assistant Secretaries but that he believed the decision to be fair because the standard used for previous decisions was unfairly high. (GAO 2001: 13)

While the OFA claims to make decisions based on precedent (since they have declined to establish specific criteria), it appears that the Assistant Secretary-Indian Affairs in actual practice is somewhat arbitrary in his granting of acknowledgement. This leaves a great deal of uncertainty in the process, and leaves the OFA open for lawsuits.

Following the GAO (2001) report, the OFA responded with "Guidance Publications" that stated how procedure would change in the Office of Federal Acknowledgement in response to the GAO report, issued in 2000, 2005, and 2008 (Gover 2000 [response to draft of GAO 2001], Cason 2005, Artman 2008). While these guidance statements made changes and suggestions for dealing with the issue of completion of the petition process in a more timely manner, they did not mention the issues related to a lack of clarity regarding meeting criteria. The OFA has attempted to make the process more transparent by publication of OFA documents on the BIA website related to the petitions of tribes, so the Proposed Finding and Final Determinations for 84a and 84b were easily accessed and downloaded by me. However, I have been unable to locate any new guidelines or clarifications of criteria that have been issued since the GAO report of 2001.

In 2005 the GAO issued another report, evaluating the OFA's response to their initial review. This report does not mention the issues of unclear criteria, it only deals with the issue of timeliness of response. The report points out that while the OFA has made internal changes to expedite the process, it is still lagging in completion of reviews of petitions:

> Even though Interior's Office of Federal Acknowledgment has increased staff resources for processing petitions and taken other actions that we recommended, as of February 4, 2005, there were 7 petitions in active status and 12 petitions in ready and waiting for active consideration status. Eight of the 12 petitions have been waiting for 7 years or more, while the 4 other petitions have been ready and waiting for active consideration since 2003. (GAO 2005)

The September 2005 Technical Assistance Letter[2] to the JBMI does not reference any updated or newly available information regarding federal acknowledgement, but only directs the JBMI to see the already existing 25 CFR 83 code:

---

2. The OFA gives advice to all petitioners. This takes the form of meetings, phone conferences, and written critiques. This letter is a follow up on a phone conference held between the JBMI (Petition 84A) and OFA staff.

[Question from tribe]

To assist the tribe in fully complying with the Federal Acknowledgement process, we are requesting that you provide the tribe with a copy of current OFA administrative, policy and guidelines which govern the authority and provisions of your office (including but not limited to the OFA solicitor's) relative to the Federal Acknowledgement process.

[Response from OFA]

OFA's procedures are set forth in 25 CFR Part 83, *Procedures for Establishing that an American Indian Group Exists as an Indian Tribe.* A copy of those regulations is enclosed as well as a copy of OFA's guidelines. (OFA 2005:3)

As previously noted, the CFR 83.7 regulations appear in Appendix 2. These guidelines do not appear to have been modified or elaborated on since the GAO (2001) report. The JBMI submitted a new petition in 2005. They were put on the Active Consideration list in 2005. The Juaneño Band of Mission Indians (JBB, or Petition 84B) requested that their petition be considered jointly with the JBMI petition. It took until November 23, 2007 for the OFA to issue a Proposed Finding. This was a finding against acknowledgement, recommending that the two groups not be granted Federal Acknowledgement. Following this issuance of the Proposed Finding was a period of time in which the petitioners and "interested third parties" could submit comment. The JBMI, the JBB, as well as several other organizations and individuals submitted comments to the proposed finding. The OFA then issued their Final Determination, in which they responded to the comments and any new information that they accepted. The Final Determination Against Acknowledgement was issued on March 15, 2011. The next section looks at the criteria that were the basis of the denial of acknowledgement.

The Finding Against Acknowledgement

The Juaneño-Acjachema were denied Federal Acknowledgement for alleged failure to meet criterion 83.7(a), 83.7(b), 83.7(c) and 83.7(e).

The criterion are listed in Table 5.2. This section goes through each of the criteria and why the OFA claims they are not adequately met. This discussion draws primarily on the Final Determination for the JBMI (referred to as JBA in OFA texts). Full texts of the Proposed Findings and Final Determinations for both groups are available on the Bureau of Indian Affairs website (www.bia.gov). Go to their "How Do I....?" section and you will find a question regarding petitioning for Federal Acknowledgement, which brings you to a page with links to regulations, PFs and FDs on prior petitions and other relevant information. A complete analysis of the Final Determination and Proposed Finding is beyond the scope of this chapter.

This chapter seeks to explain the reasons given for the denial of acknowledgement, and highlight some of the issues relating to the criterion involved. Overall, the Federal Acknowledgement process is flawed. The demand that an American Indian group prove its political and social intactness and separateness from the time of contact seems contradictory to a current federal American Indian policy that seeks to maintain obligations and acknowledgement of limited sovereignty of American Indian nations. It is suggested by some that the Federal Acknowledgement petition process was put into place to keep non-indigenous "Indian social clubs" from claiming rights as American Indian peoples, and that the process that we ended up with is too stringent and out of line with what was originally intended.

TABLE 5.2 CRITERION NOT MET: 83.7(A), 83.7(B), 83.7(C) AND 83.7(E)

a)	The petitioner has been identified as an American Indian entity on a substantially continuous basis since 1900.
b)	A predominant portion of the petitioning group comprises a distinct community and has existed as a community from historical times until the present.
c)	The petitioner has maintained political influence or authority over its members as an autonomous entity from historical times until the present.
d)	The petitioner's membership consists of individuals who descend from a historical Indian tribe or from historical Indian tribes which combined and functioned as a single autonomous political entity.

CRITERION (A): IDENTIFICATION AS A TRIBE BY EXTERNAL OBSERVERS

The Final Determination for Petition 84A states:

> The JBA petitioner does not meet the requirements of criterion 83.7(a). The evidence in the record does not demonstrate that external observers identified the petitioner, or a group from which the petitioner evolved, as an American Indian entity on a substantially continuous basis from 1900 to 1997. There are identifications of the JBA petitioner as an American Indian entity between 1997 and 2005. Because the petitioner, or a group from which the petitioner has evolved, has not been identified as an American Indian entity on a substantially continuous basis since 1900, the petitioner does not meet the requirements of criterion 83.7(a). (BIA 2011a: 11)

The JBMI submitted data from public records, newspaper reports, and other sources that referred to the Juaneño throughout this time period. The criterion states that there must be identification of the Indian entity (a group, not individuals) and that it must occur on a "substantially continuous basis." The OFA defines "substantially continuous basis" as at least every ten years (BIA 2011a:15).

The OFA found the data submitted by the JBMI as inadequate to demonstrate their existence as a political and social group identified by external observers from 1900-1997. One of the points of contention was, according to the OFA, that references were not "clearly" to a political group or separate community but were just to Indian descendants in the area. When an "entity," meaning a group that has social and political organization, is named, the OFA states that there is not proof that this Juaneño group is descendant of that political group. The following provides an example:

> The PF [Proposed Finding] concluded that the record contained no identifications of the petitioner that satisfied criterion 83.7(a) during the period from 1900 to 1949….. The PF reviewed a 1936 newspaper article by Alphonso Yorba that identifies an American Indian

entity; the article refers to "the San Juaneño Mission
Indians—a tribe that today numbers more than 300
strong and is still resident in this county" (Alphonso
Yorba, 2/1/1936). However, the PF noted that this
entity was not demonstrated to be the same entity as
either the JBA or JBB petitioner, or from which either
petitioner evolved as a group (JBA PF 2007, 42; JBB
PF 2007, 42). Therefore, this article does not identify
an entity that is the petitioner. (BIA 2011a: 17)

Throughout the Proposed Finding and the Final Determination,
the OFA agrees that the evidence does note that there are Juaneño that
are mentioned in these documents, and sometimes even that a tribe is
mentioned in the documents. Most of the critiques run that the newspaper articles or other documents only mention Juaneño individuals
and not organizations. When a tribe is mentioned, the OFA states that
there is no proof that this is "the same group." It is confusing to con-
template that a named "Juaneño Indians" tribe or "Acjachemem tribe"
or "Mission Indians" in San Juan Capistrano would somehow be different from individuals who have documented their descent from Juaneño
Indians in San Juan Capistrano today.

CRITERION (B): EXISTENCE AS A DISTINCT COMMUNITY FROM HISTORICAL TIMES TO THE PRESENT

The Federal Register notice of the Final Determination (FD) Against
Acknowledgement of the Juaneño Band of Mission Indians, Acjachemem Nation states:

> The evidence in the record demonstrates that the
> JBA petitioner did not evolve from the historical SJC
> Indian tribe as a distinct community. The FD con-
> cludes that evidence in the record indicates that a
> community of SJC Indians existed around and at the
> former SJC Mission until 1862, when a smallpox epi-
> demic killed almost half the estimated Indian popula-
> tion (88 of 200) in a period of less than 3 months. No
> evidence in the record indicates that the community
> was able to recover from this event. The petitioner, as
> it is currently constituted, consists of members whose

ancestors functioned as part of the general population of SJC residents since the mid-19th century. There is no evidence in the record that the petitioner's SJC Indian ancestors were distinct within this community after 1862, or were part of an Indian entity that evolved from the SJC Indian tribe in 1834; rather *they appear to have been Indian individuals* who became absorbed into the general, ethnically mixed population of Old Mexican/Californio families, as well as with non-SJC Indians who moved to the town prior to 1900. The totality of the evidence does not demonstrate that the petitioner's mid-19th century ancestors formed a distinct SJC Indian community within a larger Spanish-speaking, Catholic, Old Mexican/Californio community after 1862, nor does it demonstrate that the petitioner's SJC Indian ancestors formed a distinct community from which the current JBA petitioner evolved since 1862. Therefore, the JBA petitioner does not meet the requirements of criterion 83.7(b). (Echo Hawk 2011a, emphasis mine) [same for JBB]

Again, it is not that these people are not American Indian. It is not that they are not Juaneño-Acjachema. It is that they did not stay a separate group, did not avoid integration with the non-Indian population. This is an interesting aspect of the Federal Acknowledgement process. Those groups which were thoroughly colonized, which whites succeeded in destroying the separateness of, who adapted to survive by blending into the rest of the community, these groups are somehow now not owed anything by the Federal Government.

CRITERION (C):
From the Federal Register Notice:

> Criterion 83.7(c) requires that the petitioning group has maintained political influence over its members as an autonomous entity from historical times to the present. The evidence submitted for the FD, in combination with the evidence already in the record for the PF, is insufficient to satisfy the requirements of

criterion 83.7(c) for any time from 1835 to the present. (Echo Hawk 2011a) [notice for 84B is the same, Echo Hawk 2011b]

During the 1930s-1960s there was a leader of the Juaneño community named Clarence Lobo. During the time that I was conducting my fieldwork, I heard this man referred to many times as a well-known and well-respected leader in the past. During the time of his leadership, it appears that the tribe did not a have a formal constitution and did not have meetings that did things like have someone taking minutes, or in other ways create a "paper trail" of his leadership. It therefore became very difficult to prove that he was a functioning political leader, and not just an individual who has declared himself a chief. In their petition, as noted in the Proposed Finding and in the Final Determination, the JBMI submitted documentation showing that Lobo was mentioned as a local Juaneño leader in newspapers, that he was involved with the hiring of lawyers to represent the tribe, with hundreds of members signing off to be represented, and that he actively participated on local pan-Indian organizations. From the perspective of the JBMI, and many that I spoke to in the tribe during my research, he was seen as doing these things as the leader of the tribe (variously referred to as "chief" and as "Captain"). The OFA states that these claims are unsubstantiated, and that he was simply acting as an individual, not as a leader of a group (BIA 2011a: 76). The leadership of Clarence Lobo is called into question in part because he worked with pan-Indian organizations, because the greatest documentation of what he did as a leader is related to fighting for Indian claims against the federal government, and because he squabbled with the "Santa Ana group" of Indians, as well as squabbling with his own people in San Juan Capistrano. One wonders what could have possibly stood as "proof" of leadership, when acting on behalf of your people, and interacting with other organizations that would act on behalf of your people, don't count as leadership. The FD concludes:

> The FD's analysis of the information indicates that Clarence Lobo was active on behalf of pan-Indian organizations such as "the Capistrano-Santa Ana Band" and "the League of California Indians," and that he also claimed to be the leader of an organization comprised specifically of SJC Indian descendants (known by vari-

ous names including the "Capistrano Indian Band," the "San Juan Capistrano Band," and the "Juaneño Indians"). The evidence in the record supports the petitioner's assertion that some claimed SJC descendants acknowledged Lobo as their "chief," but the new information provided little information regarding a bilateral relationship between Lobo and the people who participated in the "Capistrano Indian Band." It also provided little evidence of the members of the group contacting Lobo for reasons other than those related to the claims issue. The evidence submitted did not provide evidence of leadership or internal processes used to influence or control the behavior of the petitioner's members in significant respects. The evidence is insufficient to demonstrate political authority or influence over a group of petitioner's ancestors or members for this time period, and the negative findings of the PF for the time period 1934-1964 are unchanged. (BIA 2011a:81)

CRITERION (E): DESCENT FROM A HISTORICAL INDIAN TRIBE

Criterion 83.7(e) requires that the petitioner's members descend from a historical Indian tribe. According to the OFA, the available evidence shows that only 61% of the JMBI's 1,940 members demonstrated descent from the historical Indian tribe at San Juan Capistrano Mission. (BIA 2011a) For the JBB, 84B petitioner, the OFA claimed that only 53% (241 of 455) of the members demonstrated descent (Echo Hawk 2011b). The GOA (2001) report cited above notes a case in which a tribe had 48% of its membership that demonstrated descent, and the Assistant Secretary declared them federally recognized, and said that the criterion for percent membership was "too high" (GAO 2001:12). Clearly there is no standard being applied consistently to all petitioners.

Overall, the Final Determination (BIA 2011a, see also BIA 2011b) does not say that the petitioning groups are not American Indian, it does not even say that they are not Juaneño. What it says is that they have not maintained a separate community since colonial times, and that they have not maintained an intact political system since colonial times. Put another way: they were successfully colonized. So, because the Spanish and then the encroaching whites succeeded in taking their lands, dispersing their people, destroying their political system and social system, they are not owed anything by the U.S. government?

Federal Acknowledgement is supposed to entail ongoing treaty obligations to the indigenous people of the territory that came to be the U.S. It also has been characterized as ongoing payment for the land and resources we as a nation have. To suggest that American Indian groups have to have maintained an intact community and an intact functioning political organization in order to qualify for such compensation is simply ludicrous.

So, those groups which resisted, or which remained somewhat isolated, often because they were on or were forced onto lands that had few resources that the whites would want, were left alone and are more likely to be able to have Federal Acknowledgement. Those groups which were in areas rich in resources, or which were travel corridors (SJC is both) were more likely to be fully colonized, swept into the social, political and labor systems of the region, and thus are less likely to have, or qualify for, Federal Acknowledgement.

No, the Juaneño did not remain living in one community in SJC, they went out to the ranches and fields and cities and found work. No, they did not marry only Juaneños, they married whites and Spanish and formed families just like other people.

The criterion of the Federal Acknowledgement process make it very difficult for American Indians to become federally recognized. One begins to question the purpose of the Federal Acknowledgement process. If the purpose were to meet the ongoing obligations to the indigenous people from whom the land we are living on was stolen, taken by force, or bought at insanely low prices; then the criteria that they ought to have maintained an intact, separate, community politically and socially, ought not to be part of the determining criteria.

Everything is against this having been so for California Indians, particularly those who were on land where there were resources or routes of travel. From the Spanish missionaries, to the 1850s vagrancy laws, to the boarding school policies, to economic conditions that forced people to move to find work; everything has worked against the Indians of California, and the Juaneño-Acjachema in particular, from remaining intact as a community. It is simply outrageous that they should now be denied Federal Acknowledgement and the few benefits that entails because they were not able to prove their existence as a separate community and political entity.

Reaction to the Denial of Federal Acknowledgement

JBMI tribal chair Anthony Rivera has stated that he will pursue all avenues available to attain Federal Acknowledgement. The following is from the local paper, the Capistrano Dispatch:

> "The Tribe is very disappointed that the AS-IA [Assistant Secretary-Indian Affairs] and the Office of Federal Acknowledgment (OFA) failed to properly evaluate the thousands of pieces of evidence the Tribe had presented. This is a great and continued injustice to the Acjachemen Tribe," Rivera said in a statement. "Based on the thousands of pages of credible evidence, the Tribe will move ahead over the next stage to evaluate the OFA's conclusions and prepare to appeal the inaccurate decision." (Volzke 2011)

The process of petitioning for Federal Acknowledgment has had a significant divisive effect on the community. In the 1990s, there were disputed elections and two separate factionings of the tribe, reportedly at least somewhat related to the Federal Acknowledgement process. Accusations continue to abound between factions as to supposed involvement with "casino interests." In the Final Determination of Petition 84A, there is discussion of comments on the Proposed Finding in which a third faction, designated by the OFA as an "interested party" (JMBI-IP) accused the JBMI of having contracts with casino interests. This accusation was denied by the JBMI and the OFA found no evidence of such contracts. While I was doing my research with the community 2000-2003, working primarily with the JBMI, discussions of the spilt with this "interested party" always included the accusation of his being in talks with casino investors. I have no data on whether any group was or is making deals with casino investors, but the in-group out-group identification seems to have expanded to include not just "not Juaneño " but "in with casino interests" as marking one as "out-group."

In 2008, there was upheaval in the JBMI tribe due to the dis-enrollment of people from the tribe as part of the petitioning process. During the process of petitioning for Federal Acknowledgement, the tribal government of the JBMI had to make some difficult decisions regarding membership. They had to demonstrate, to very strict standards, that the majority of their enrolled members were descendants from the Juaneños who were living at or near the Mission San Juan Capistrano in 1834. It is not surprising that everyone who believes themselves to be Juaneño was not able to do this.

In a discussion with a member of the tribe's leadership, I was told of one family, whom I have known for years and who has been involved in the tribe for decades, and who were some of those who put in long hours working for the tribe and for Federal Acknowledgement, were not able to document their genealogical descent from the Juaneño who had been at the Mission in 1834. The disenrollment of this family, and others, was a difficult and heart-wrenching decision. This comes back to the criterion of an "intact community." The OFA distinguished between those who were Juaneño and stayed in San Juan Capistrano, and those who left SJC, even though they stayed in Orange County, they were not considered part of the "community" as defined by the OFA (BIA 2011a:12).

This disenrollment of members, many of whom had been involved in the community for a very long time, led to significant conflict and bad feelings toward the current leadership of the JBMI. The comment to a newspaper article about the Final Determination Against below is somewhat typical of responses:[3]

> As one of those "Juaneños" with both a BIA roll number and verification of blood percentage that was left off the "list" …[I] stand proud in knowing that we are true members and cannot be told or dictated to from a few board members of exclusion in the tribe. (Locally Grown 2011)

The resentment of some of those who were dis-enrolled is apparent in the quote from "Locally Grown" above. It is also completely understandable. What right, after all, do others have to tell you what your ethnicity is? Little right, one might think. However, ethnic identity is a socially negotiated status. Acceptance by the ethnic group as "one of us" is part of the identity process. And, for American Indians, their social construction of ethnic identity is entangled with the legal identification by the Bureau of Indian Affairs as American Indian, and is also entangled with the (technically and legally separate) identification of

---

3. Only "somewhat typical" in that this is in fact a mild response. The level of hostility is high in comments to newspaper articles about the Final Determination.

a group as a legally identified tribe, to whom the federal government acknowledges ongoing treaty obligations (Federal Acknowledgement).

The three processes and identifications are often conflated in discussions and self-identification. Locally Grown's comment states that he/she has a BIA card and verified blood quantum, yet he/she was apparently unable to prove genealogical descent from a Juaneño at the Mission in 1834, or unable to produce documentation in a timely manner to meet the deadline for submission of the Petition materials. Criteria to prove oneself Indian for a BIA card is not the same criteria as is being used by the BIA in the Juaneño's petition process, moreover the BIA criteria is itself often inconsistent.[4] Moreover, the process of identification as a tribe that the U.S. government has treaty obligations to is another set of criteria altogether. Many people, following the Federal Determination Against, are talking about their continued identity as Juaneño. Their need to state this is wrapped up in this conflation of "ongoing treaty obligations" [Federal Acknowledgement] and identity as American Indian individuals. Unfortunately the linkage of the two is strong, so that Juaneños now might face even stronger criticisms from both whites and other American Indians about their claims to American Indian identity.

Some people criticize the current political leadership of the JMBI as hostile. In June of 2011, I interviewed Juaneño community member Robert Bracemontes,[5] who also uses the name Bob Black Crow:

> I've been to meetings with Anthony [Rivera], I've sat down with Anthony and talked to him for a couple of hours. I feel that that's a very restrictive and fascist environment. His meetings are conducted all in the

4. In the spring of 1998 I was in the JBMI offices working on the organization of a breast cancer screening outreach event. One of the tribe's staff people was also working, and I overheard a phone conversation she had with BIA staff. She had submitted genealogical evidence for a brother and sister, to get their BIA cards. The submitted genealogies for the brother and sister were identical. They both received BIA cards identifying them as American Indian, but each sibling was designated as a having a different blood quantum, or as being different percentage American Indian. I asked her about their response to this when she got off the phone. She said that they didn't have an answer, only that different staff people at the BIA had probably worked on the two cases separately. This calls into question standards for designation of American Indian identity and blood quantum by the BIA.
5. Robert Bracemontes is a writer, having had a column in an LA newspaper in the past. I met him through his participation in Juaneño community events, including the yearly Ancestors Walk described in the opening of this book.

name of "what we say in here will stay in here, and we will not share this with anyone outside of our group" whether they are native or not native, and particularly if they are in the other group, we don't want them to know this.

All knowledge is political, and I believe that when we restrict people from information and knowledge, that's political. And I think in particular that Anthony is doing that... I don't think it's my place to say that it's because of a selfish reason or a greedy reason, but it may also be that a reason [is] because they want to fulfill the criteria, so you get into this Catch-22. Let's fulfill the criteria, oh, but that means that we have to have a purge, well then that means that Robert Bracemontes goes [because] in our opinion—and that's another opinion—he can't prove his lineage back. And then we get back to the whole idea of evidence, and now I feel defensive, because you have to produce evidence, like I committed some kind of crime. So now I'm a criminal in my own community. And I have to present this evidence that in fact I'm not the criminal, I'm not an outsider, that I am Juaneño even with my own and that's ludicrous. (Bracemontes/Bob Black Crow 2011)

Bob Black Crow mentions a "catch-22" and this is exactly what this "purge" as he puts it, turned out to be. As part of the effort to meet the criteria for Federal Acknowledgement, the JBMI dis-enrolled all those members that were unable to prove their genealogical descent from the Juaneño who were documented as present in SJC in 1834. In the next round of paperwork with the OFA, they submit this new membership list. In the Final Determination, the OFA states the following:

The 2009 membership list dramatically differs from its [Petition 84A's] prior membership lists, with the removal of 928 adults and the addition of 1,244 new people. In making such dramatic changes to its membership list, the petitioner has created a new problem in that the composition of the group the list now describes is very different than the group described in the materials submitted for the PF. The explanation of the membership changes given by the petitioner does not account for the previous involvement of a number of now-excluded families and individuals, some of whom were active in the MIF [Mission Indian Federation], during the Lobo era, and in the JBM and JBA for many years. It also does not explain the sudden addition to the roll of over 800 individuals who had had no documented interaction with the petitioner until their names appeared on the 2009 membership list. ...The contemporary JBA group so differs from the group described in the PF that the descriptions, analyses, and evaluations of community previously advanced by the petitioner in the materials submitted for the PF do not apply to the group as it is now constituted. (BIA 2011a: 35-36)

So, by attempting to meet the criteria for documented descent from the very small group of Juaneños who were present at the Mission in the 1800s, the JBMI, according to the OFA, has undermined their documentation of themselves as a community. It is a no-win situation for the Juaneño.

Beyond Federal Acknowledgement: Indigenous Rights

The Federal Acknowledgement process is flawed in several ways. The level of proof of existence as an intact community and political entity is very high. Moreover, the level of proof required seems to vary on a case-by-case basis. The OFA has to this date, still not clarified specific criteria nor specific cutoffs for things like percent of members with demonstrated descent. They appear to rely on precedent when it suits them, and ignore it when it does not.

Moreover, the participation in the petitioning process has caused rift after rift in the Juaneño–Acjachema community. This may be in part due to the potential for profit in a casino if the tribe were to have gotten Federal Acknowledgement. However, the possibility of a casino caused many in the community of San Juan Capistrano as well as the larger Southern California community, to argue against the Juaneño gaining Federal Acknowledgement.

The JBMI has stated that it will further pursue Federal Acknowledgement. I believe that they will go as far as a lawsuit, so it may be many more years before the issue is fully resolved. When it is, and if they don't get Federal Acknowledgement, they as a tribe and as Juaneño individuals will have to find some way to go on as a community and as Juaneño in a complex, multi-cultural world. My hope for them is that they can continue to express their Juaneño identity, and that the families and former friends that have been torn apart by the political rifts, disenrollments, and other events of recent years, will find a way to mend the bridges between them.

In September 2007 the United Nations' General Assembly adopted a Declaration of the Rights of Indigenous Peoples. One-hundred and forty-four of the nations in the General Assembly voted in favor of this Declaration; Australia, Canada, New Zealand, and the United States all voted against its adoption. All four of these are nations whose majority population is of European descent, and who took the land from an indigenous people who remain a disempowered minority in the nations. It might be time to for unacknowledged tribes in the United States to dispense with the Federal Acknowledgement process and pursue their rights as indigenous peoples on the world stage.

appendix1

TABLE A.1

American Indians in California	California
Total California Population	**37,253,956**
American Indian and Alaska Native alone	362,801
White; American Indian and Alaska Native	208,833
Black or African American; American Indian and Alaska Native	31,146
American Indian and Alaska Native; Asian	15,072
American Indian and Alaska Native; Native Hawaiian and Other Pacific Islander	2,321
American Indian and Alaska Native; Some Other Race	29,519
White; Black or African American; American Indian and Alaska Native	31,949
White; American Indian and Alaska Native; Asian	13,195
White; American Indian and Alaska Native; Native Hawaiian and Other Pacific Islander	2,109
White; American Indian and Alaska Native; Some Other Race	8,873
Black or African American; American Indian and Alaska Native; Asian	2,129
Black or African American; American Indian and Alaska Native; Native Hawaiian and Other Pacific Islander	427
Black or African American; American Indian and Alaska Native; Some Other Race	1,532
American Indian and Alaska Native; Asian; Native Hawaiian and Other Pacific Islander	739

American Indian and Alaska Native; Asian; Some Other Race	1,105
American Indian and Alaska Native; Native Hawaiian and Other Pacific Islander; Some Other Race	361
White; Black or African American; American Indian and Alaska Native; Asian	4,341
White; Black or African American; American Indian and Alaska Native; Native Hawaiian and Other Pacific Islander	616
White; Black or African American; American Indian and Alaska Native; Some Other Race	1,785
White; American Indian and Alaska Native; Asian; Native Hawaiian and Other Pacific Islander	1,567
White; American Indian and Alaska Native; Asian; Some Other Race	546
White; American Indian and Alaska Native; Native Hawaiian and Other Pacific Islander; Some Other Race	124
Black or African American; American Indian and Alaska Native; Asian; Native Hawaiian and Other Pacific Islander	227
Black or African American; American Indian and Alaska Native; Asian; Some Other Race	166
Black or African American; American Indian and Alaska Native; Native Hawaiian and Other Pacific Islander; Some Other Race	31
American Indian and Alaska Native; Asian; Native Hawaiian and Other Pacific Islander; Some Other Race	76
White; Black or African American; American Indian and Alaska Native; Asian; Native Hawaiian and Other Pacific Islander	1,135
White; Black or African American; American Indian and Alaska Native; Asian; Some Other Race	216

White; Black or African American; American Indian and Alaska Native; Native Hawaiian and Other Pacific Islander; Some Other Race	59
White; American Indian and Alaska Native; Asian; Native Hawaiian and Other Pacific Islander; Some Other Race	87
Black or African American; American Indian and Alaska Native; Asian; Native Hawaiian and Other Pacific Islander; Some Other Race	15
White; Black or African American; American Indian and Alaska Native; Asian; Native Hawaiian and Other Pacific Islander; Some Other Race	123
Total	723,225

(Adapted from: 2010 Census Redistricting Data (Public Law 94-171) Summary File; CALIFORNIA: RACE)

appendix 2

25CFR 83

§83.1 Definitions [relevant excerpts]

Community means any group of people which can demonstrate that consistent interactions and significant social relationships exist within its membership and that its members are differentiated from and identified as distinct from nonmembers. *Community* must be understood in the context of the history, geography, culture, and social organization of the group.

§83.7 Mandatory Criteria for Federal Acknowledgment
The mandatory criteria are:
(a) The petitioner has been identified as an American Indian entity on a substantially continuous basis since 1900. Evidence that the group's character as an Indian entity has from time to time been denied shall not be considered to be conclusive evidence that this criterion has not been met. Evidence to be relied upon in determining a group's Indian identity may include one or a combination of the following, as well as other evidence of identification by other than the petitioner itself or its members.
   (1) Identification as an Indian entity by Federal authorities.
   (2) Relationships with State governments based on identification of the group as Indian.
   (3) Dealings with a county, parish, or other local government in a relationship based on the group's Indian identity.
   (4) Identification as an Indian entity by anthropologists, historians, and/or other scholars.
   (5) Identification as an Indian entity in newspapers and books.

(6) Identification as an Indian entity in relationships with Indian tribes or with national, regional, or state Indian organizations.

(b) A predominant portion of the petitioning group comprises a distinct community and has existed as a community from historical times until the present.

    (1) This criterion may be demonstrated by some combination of the following evidence and/or other evidence that the petitioner meets the definition of *community* set forth in § 83.1:

        (i) Significant rates of marriage within the group, and/or, as may be culturally required, patterned out-marriages with other Indian populations.

        (ii) Significant social relationships connecting individual members.

        (iii) Significant rates of informal social interaction which exist broadly among the members of a group.

        (iv) A significant degree of shared or cooperative labor or other economic activity among the membership.

        (v) Evidence of strong patterns of discrimination or other social distinctions by non-members.

        (vi) Shared sacred or secular ritual activity encompassing most of the group.

        (vii) Cultural patterns shared among a significant portion of the group that are different from those of the non-Indian populations with whom it interacts. These patterns must function as more than a symbolic identification of the group as Indian. They may include, but are not limited to, language, kinship organization, or religious beliefs and practices.

        (viii) The persistence of a named, collective Indian identity continuously over a period of more than 50 years, notwithstanding changes in name.

        (ix) A demonstration of historical political influence under the criterion in § 83.7(c) shall be evidence for demonstrating historical community.

    (2) A petitioner shall be considered to have provided sufficient evidence of community at a given point in time if evidence is provided to demonstrate any one of the following:

        (i) More than 50 percent of the members reside in a geographical area exclusively or almost exclusively composed of members of the group, and the balance of the group maintains consistent interaction with some members of the community;

(ii) At least 50 percent of the marriages in the group are between members of the group;

(iii) At least 50 percent of the group members maintain distinct cultural patterns such as, but not limited to, language, kinship organization, or religious beliefs and practices;

(iv) There are distinct community social institutions encompassing most of the members, such as kinship organizations, formal or informal economic cooperation, or religious organizations; or

(v) The group has met the criterion in § 83.7(c) using evidence described in§ 83.7(c)(2).

(c) The petitioner has maintained political influence or authority over its members as an autonomous entity from historical times until the present.

(1) This criterion may be demonstrated by some combination of the evidence listed below and/or by other evidence that the petitioner meets the definition of political influence or authority in § 83.1.

(i) The group is able to mobilize significant numbers of members and significant resources from its members for group purposes.

(ii) Most of the membership considers issues acted upon or actions taken by group leaders or governing bodies to be of importance.

(iii) There is widespread knowledge, communication and involvement in political processes by most of the group's members.

(iv) The group meets the criterion in § 83.7(b) at more than a minimal level.

(v) There are internal conflicts which show controversy over valued group goals, properties, policies, processes and/or decisions.

(2) A petitioning group shall be considered to have provided sufficient evidence to demonstrate the exercise of political influence or authority at a given point in time by

demonstrating that group leaders and/or other mechanisms exist or existed which:

(i) Allocate group resources such as land, residence rights and the like on a consistent basis.

(ii) Settle disputes between members or subgroups by mediation or other means on a regular basis;

(iii) Exert strong influence on the behavior of individual members, such as the establishment or maintenance of norms and the enforcement of sanctions to direct or control behavior;

(iv) Organize or influence economic subsistence activities among the members, including shared or cooperative labor.

(3) A group that has met the requirements in paragraph 83.7(b)(2) at a given point in time shall be considered to have provided sufficient evidence to meet this criterion at that point in time.

(d) A copy of the group's present governing document including its membership criteria. In the absence of a written document, the petitioner must provide a statement describing in full its membership criteria and current governing procedures.

(e) The petitioner's membership consists of individuals who descend from a historical Indian tribe or from historical Indian tribes which combined and functioned as a single autonomous political entity.

(1) Evidence acceptable to the Secretary which can be used for this purpose includes but is not limited to:

(i) Rolls prepared by the Secretary on a descendancy basis for purposes of distributing claims money, providing allotments, or other purposes;

(ii) State, Federal, or other official records or evidence identifying present members or ancestors of present members as being descendants of a historical tribe or tribes that combined as a political entity.

(iii) Church, school, and other similar enrollment records identifying present members or ancestors of present members as being descendants of a historical tribe or tribes that combined and functioned as a single autonomous political entity.

      (iv) Affidavits of recognition by tribal elders, leaders, or the tribal governing body identifying present members or ancestors of present members as being descendants of a historical tribe or tribes that combined and functioned as a single autonomous political entity.

      (v) Other records or evidence identifying present members or ancestors of present members as being descendants of a historical tribe or tribes that combined and functioned as a single autonomous political entity.

  (2) The petitioner must provide an official membership list, separately certified by the group's governing body, of all known current members of the group. This list must include each member's full name (including maiden name), date of birth, and current residential address. The petitioner must also provide a copy of each available former list of members based on the group's own defined criteria, as well as a statement describing the circumstances surrounding the preparation of the current list and, insofar as possible, the circumstances surrounding the preparation of former lists.

(f) The membership of the petitioning group is composed principally of persons who are not members of any acknowledged North American Indian tribe. However, under certain conditions a petitioning group may be acknowledged even if its membership is composed principally of persons whose names have appeared on rolls of, or who have been otherwise associated with, an acknowledged Indian tribe. The conditions are that the group must establish that it has functioned throughout history until the present as a separate and autonomous Indian tribal entity, that its members do not maintain a bilateral political relationship with the acknowledged tribe, and that its members have provided written confirmation of their membership in the petitioning group.

(g) Neither the petitioner nor its members are the subject of congressional legislation that has expressly terminated or forbidden the Federal relationship.

appendix 3

25 CFR PART 83 PROCEDURES FOR ESTABLISHING THAT AN AMERICAN INDIAN GROUP EXISTS AS AN INDIAN TRIBE

83.7 Mandatory criteria for Federal Acknowledgment

The mandatory criteria are:

(a) The petitioner has been identified as an American Indian entity on a substantially continuous basis since 1900.

(b) A predominant portion of the petitioning group comprises a distinct community and has existed as a community from historical times until the present.

(c) The petitioner has maintained political influence or authority over its members as an autonomous entity from historical times until the present.

(d) A copy of the group's present governing document including its membership criteria. In the absence of a written document, the petitioner must provide a statement describing in full its membership criteria and current governing procedures.

(e) The petitioner's membership consists of individuals who descend from a historical Indian tribe or from historian Indian tribes which combined and functioned as a single autonomous political entity.

(f) The membership of the petitioning group is composed principally of persons who are not members of any acknowledged North American Indian tribe.

(g) Neither the petitioner nor its members are the subject of congressional legislation that has expressly terminated or forbidden the Federal relationship.

The seven criteria are presented here in abbreviated form. For the complete text of each criterion, please refer to 25 CFR Part 83.

references

Anderson, G. E., W. H. Ellison and R. F. Heizer
1978. *Treaty Making and Treaty Rejection by the Federal Government in California, 1850-1982.* Ballena Press, Socorro: New Mexico.

Artman, Carl
2008. *Office of Federal Acknowledgment; Guidance and Direction Regarding Internal Procedures.* Department of the Interior, Bureau of Indian Affairs. Federal Register, Vol. 73, No. 101. Friday, May 23, 2008, Notices: 30146-30148.

Bancroft, Hubert. H.
1884. *The History of California,* Vol. 1 San Francisco: The History Company.
1886. *The History of California,* Vol. 4. San Francisco: The History Company.

Bean, Lowell, ed.
1992. *California Indian Shamanism.* Socorro, New Mexico: Ballena Press.

Bean, Lowell J. and Florence Shipek
1978. Luiseño. In California, R. F. Heizer, ed. *Handbook of North American Indians,* vol. 8. W. C. Sturtevant, general editor. Washington, D.C.: Smithsonian Institution: 550-563.

Blu, Karen I.
1980. *The Lumbee Problem: The Making of an American Indian People.* Cambridge: Cambridge University Press.

Bracemontes, Robert/Bob Black Crow
2011. Interview conducted by author, June 12, 2011. Irvine, CA.

Brophy, William W., Sophie D. Aberle, W. W. Keeler, et al.
1966. *The Indian: America's Unfinished Business: Report of the Commission on the Rights, Liberties and Responsibilities of the American Indian.* Norman: University of Oklahoma Press.

Bureau of Indian Affairs

    1933. Copy of the Roll Approved in 1933 Listing the Indians of California qualified under sec. 1 of the Act of May 18, 1928. Microfilm on file, National Archives, Pacific Southwest Region, Laguna Niguel.

    2007a. Proposed Finding Against Acknowledgement of The Juaneño Band of Mission Indians, Acjachemem Nation. (Petitioner #84A). Department of Interior, Bureau of Indian Affairs, Office of Federal Acknowledgement. http://www.bia.gov/idc/groups/xofa/documents/text/idc-001619.pdf

    2007b. Proposed Finding Against Acknowledgement of The Juaneño Band of Mission Indians. (Petition 84b). Department of Interior, Bureau of Indian Affairs, Office of Federal Acknowledgement.

    2011a. Echo Hawk Issues Final Determinations Against Acknowledgement of the Juaneño Band of Mission Indians, Acjachema Nation. [Petition 84A] Press Release. Office of the Secretary-Indian Affairs, U.S. Department of the Interior. March 11, 2011.

    2011a. Echo Hawk Issues Final Determinations Against Acknowledgement of the Juaneño Band of Mission Indians. [Petition 84B] Press Release. Office of the Secretary-Indian Affairs, U.S. Department of the Interior. March 11, 2011.

    2011a. Final Determination Against Acknowledgement of The Juaneño Band of Mission Indians, Acjachemem Nation. (Petitioner #84A).

    Department of Interior, Bureau of Indian Affairs, Office of Federal Acknowledgement. http://www.bia.gov/idc/groups/xofa/documents/text/idc013298.pdf.

    2011b. Final Determination Against Acknowledgement of the Juaneño Band of Mission Indians. (Petition 84B). Department of Interior, Bureau of Indian Affairs, Office of Federal Acknowledgement. http://www.bia.gov/idc/groups/xofa/documents/text/idc013299.pdf.

California Cities for Self Reliance

    2011 (accessed). California Cities for Self Reliance/Joint Powers Authority, http://www.californiacitiesforselfreliance.com/about.html.

Cason, James

2005. Office of Federal Acknowledgment; Reports and Guidance Documents; Availability, etc. Department of the Interior. Bureau of Indian Affairs. Federal Register, Vol. 70, No. 61 Thursday, March 31, 2005, Notices: 16513-16516.

Census Bureau

2000. United States Census 2000. American Factfinder.

2005-2009. American Community Survey, www.census.gov

Champagne, Dwayne

2000. Talk given in UCI Cross-Cultural Center on American Indian Law.

Clarke, Adele E. and Virginia L. Olesen

1999. Revising, Diffracting, Acting. Introduction to *Revisioning Women, Health and Healing: Feminist, Cultural and Technoscience Perspectives*. A. E. Clarke and V. L. Olesen, editors. New York: Routledge.

Columbia Electronic Encyclopedia

2003. Yerba Buena. Plants. *The Columbia Electronic Encyclopedia*. Columbia University Press.

http://reference.allrefer.com/encyclopedia/Y/yerbabue.html

Cook, Sherburne Friend

1940. Population Trends Among the California Mission Indians. *Ibero-Americana:* 17, Los Angeles: University of California Press.

1941. The Mechanism and Extent of Dietary Adaptation Among Certain Groups of California and Nevada Indians. *Ibero-Americana: 18*, Los Angeles: University of California Press.

1971a [1943]. Conflict Between the California Indian and White Civilization. In *The California Indians,* 2nd ed. R. F. Heizer and M. A. Whipple, eds. Los Angeles: University of California Press.

1971b [1943]. Migration and Urbanization of the Indians in California, In *The California Indians,* 2nd ed. R. F. Heizer and M. A. Whipple, eds. Los Angeles: University of California Press.

1976a The Population of California Indians: 1769-1970. Los Angeles: University of California Press.

1976b. The Conflict Between the California Indian and White Civilization. Berkeley: University of California Press.

Costo, Rupert and Jeanette Henry Costo, eds.
     1987. *The Mission Indians of California: A Legacy of Genocide.*
     The Indian Historian Press, for The American Indian Histori-
     cal Society Ann Arbor, Michigan: Braun-Brumfield.

Cowan, Robert G.
     1977. *Ranchos of California.* Los Angeles: Historical Society of
     Southern California.

Darian-Smith, Eve
     2004. *New Capitalists: Law Politics and Identity Surrounding
     Casino Gaming on Native American Land.* Belmont, CA:
     Thompson/Wadsworth Publishing.

Davis-Floyd, Robbie E.
     1987. The Technological Model of Birth. *Journal of American
     Folklore* 100 (398): 479-95.
     1992. *Birth as an American Rite of Passage.* Los Angeles: Univer-
     sity of California Press.

Davis-Floyd, Robbie E. and Carolyn F. Sargent, eds.
     1997. *Childbirth and Authoritative Knowledge: Cross-Cultural
     Perspectives.* Los Angeles: University of California Press.

Dias, Christine Marie
     1996. San Juan Capistrano Mission Records: Juaneño Conver-
     sion and Risk Minimization. Dissertation, California State
     University, Long Beach.

Dorrington, Lafayette
     1927. Letter to the Commissioner of Indian Affairs. January 20.
     California Consolidated Files, Record Group 75, Records of
     Bureau of Indian Affairs, Central Classified Files, 1907-1939,
     GSA 310/1927.

Dundes, Lauren, ed.
     2003. *The Manner Born: Birth Rites in Cross-Cultural Perspec-
     tive.* New York: AltaMira Press/Rowman & Littlefield Publish-
     ers.

Earle, David D. and Stephen O'Neil
     1994. An Ethnohistoric Analysis of Population, Settlement,
     and Social Organization in Coastal Orange County at the End
     of the Late Prehistoric Period. Series Newport Coast Archaeo-
     logical Project. Costa Mesa, CA: The Keith Companies.

Eakins, Pamela, ed.
>   1986. *The American Way of Birth*. Philadelphia: Temple University Press.

Echo Hawk, Larry
>   2011a. "Final Determination Against Acknowledgement of the Juaneño Band of Mission Indians, Acjachemem Nation." Department of the Interior; Bureau of Indian Affairs. Federal Register, Vol. 76: No. 54. Monday, March 21, 2011. Notices: 15337-15338. Washington, D.C.: United States Government Printing Office.
>   2011b. "Final Determination Against Acknowledgment of the Juaneño Band of Mission Indians," Federal Register, Vol. 76, No. 54, Monday, March 21, 2011, Notices: 15335-15337. Washington, D.C.: United States Government Printing Office.

Engelhardt, Zephyrin OFM
>   1922. San Juan Capistrano Mission. Series: Missions and Missionaries in California. Los Angeles, Santa Barbara: Mission Santa Barbara.

Field, Les W.
>   1999. Complications and Collaborations: Anthropologists and the Unacknowledged Tribes of California. *Current Anthropology* 40(2): 193-209.

Fogel, David
>   1988. *Junipero Serra, the Vatican and Enslavement Theology*. San Francisco: Ism Press.

Fraser, Gertrude J.
>   1995. Modern Bodies, Modern Minds: Midwifery and Reproductive Change in an African-American Community. In *Conceiving the New World Order: The Global Politics of Reproduction*. Ginsberg, Faye D. and Rayna Rapp, eds. 42-58. Los Angeles: University of California Press.

Geiger, Maynard
>   1952. Reply of Mission San Antonio to questionnaire of the Spanish Government in 1812 concerning the native culture of the California Mission Indians. *The Americas*. 10(2):211-117.

Gifford, E. W.
>   1971. California Balanophagy. In R. F. Heizer and A. M. Whipple, eds. *The California Indians: A Source Book*. 2nd edition, Los Angeles: University of California Press.

Goldberg, Carole
    2004. Questions and Answers About PL 280. Electronic
    Document. http://www.tribal-institute.org/articles/goldberg.
    htm. Accessed Oct. 23, 2004.
Goffman, Erving.
    1959. *The Presentation of Self in Everyday Life.* Garden City:
    Anchor.
    1967. *Interaction Ritual.* New York: Doubleday.
Gover, Kevin
    2000. Changes in the Internal Processing of Federal Acknowl-
    edgment Petitions. Department of the Interior. Bureau of
    Indian Affairs. Federal Register, Vol. 65, No. 29, Friday, Febru-
    ary 11, 2000. Notices: 7052-7053.
Guest, Francis Florian O.F.M.
    1983. Cultural Perspectives on California Mission Life. Southern
    California Quarterly Historical Society of Southern California.
Harrington, John P.
    1934. Chinigchinich: A New Original Version of Boscana's
    Historical Account of the San Juan Capistrano Indians of
    Southern California. City of Washington: Published by the
    Smithsonian Institution (June 27, 1934). [Smithsonian In-
    stitution publication 1255] 1986 Southern California/Basin.
    Ethnographic Field Notes, Pt. 3. National Anthropological
    Archives, Smithsonian Institution, Washington D.C. [Avail on
    Microfilm Kraus International Publications, Milkwood, N.Y.]
Heizer, R. F., ed.
    1972. The Eighteen Unratified Treaties of 1851-1852 between
    the California Indians and the United States Government.
    Berkeley: University of California Archeological Research Center.
    1974. *The Destruction of the California Indians.* Santa Barbara:
    Peregrine. Smith, Inc.
Heizer, R. F. and M. A. Whipple
    1971. *The California Indians: A Sourcebook.* Los Angeles: Uni-
    versity of California Press.
Hurtado, Albert L.
    1988. *Indian Survival on the California Frontier.* New Haven:
    Yale University Press.

Jackson, Helen Hunt and Abbot Kinney

1994. On the Conditions and Needs of the Missions Indians of California. Appendix XV [1883 report] in *A Century of Dishonor: A Sketch of the United States Government's Dealings with Some of the Indian Tribes*, by Helen Hunt Jackson, Pp. 458-514. New York: Indian Head Books.

Jackson, Robert H. and Edward Castillo,

1995. *Indians, Franciscans, and Spanish Colonization: The Impact of the Mission System on California Indians.* Albuquerque: University of New Mexico Press.

Johnson, John R., Dinah J. Crawford, and Stephen O'Neil.

1998. The Ethnohistoric Basis for Cultural Affiliation in the Camp Pendleton Marine Base Area: Contributions to Luiseño and Juaneño Ethnohistory Based on Mission Register Research. Report prepared for Los Angeles District, U.S. Army Corps of Engineers. Science Applications International Corporation, Santa Barbara.

Johnson, John R., and Stephen O'Neil

2001. Descendants of Native Communities in the Vicinity of Marine Corps Base Camp Pendleton: An Ethnohistoric Study of Luiseño and Juaneño Cultural Affiliation. Santa Barbara: Science Applications International Corporation.

Johnson-Dodds, Kimberly

2002. Early Laws and Policies Related to California Indians. Prepared at the request of Senator John L. Burton. Sacramento, CA: California Research Bureau, California State Library.

Jordan, Brigitte

1980. *Birth in Four Cultures.* Montreal, Canada: Eden Press Women's Publications.

1997. Authoritative Knowledge and Its Construction. In *Childbirth and Authoritative Knowledge: Cross-Cultural Perspectives.* Robbie E. Davis-Floyd and Carolyn F. Sargent, eds. Los Angeles: University of California Press.

Kay, Margarita Artschwager

1982. *Anthropology of Human Birth.* Philadelphia: F. A. Davis Company.

1982. Writing and Ethnography of Birth," Introduction to in M. A. Kay, ed. *The Anthropology of Human Birth.* Philadelphia: F. A. Davis Company.

Kelly, Isabel

> 1965. *Folk Practices in North Mexico.* Austin: University of Texas Press.

Kroeber, A. L

> 1971a [1951]. Elements of Culture in Native California. In R. F. Heizer and A. M. Whipple, eds. *The California Indians: A Source Book.* 2nd edition, Los Angeles: University of California Press.
>
> 1971b. The Food Problem in California. In R. F. Heizer and A. M. Whipple, eds. *The California Indians: A Source Book.* 2nd edition, Los Angeles: University of California Press.
>
> 1976 [1925]. *Handbook of the Indians of California.* New York: Dover Publications, Inc. [originally published as: Bulletin No. 78, Bureau of American Ethnology, Smithsonian Institution.]

Locally Grown

> 2011. Comment on article, "Updated: No Federal Recognition for Juaneño" by Jenna Chandler, March 17, 2011, San Juan Capistrano Dispatch, published online: http://sanjuancapistrano. patch.com/articles/ no-federal-recognition-for-juaneno.

Merrit, E. B.

> 1927. Letter to Lafayette A. Dorrington, May 26, California Consolidated Files, Record Group 75, Records of Bureau of Indian Affairs, Central Classified Files, 1907-1939, GSA 310/1927.

Mitford, Jessica

> 1992. *The American Way of Birth.* New York: Penguin Books/ Dutton.

Nixon, Richard

> 1970. President Nixon, Special Message on Indian Affairs, July 8, 1970. Address to Congress. Electronic Document. http://www.epa.gov/indian/pdfs/nixon70.pdf, accessed Oct. 23, 2002.

O'Brien, Sharon

> 1989. American Indian Tribal Governments. Norman: University of Oklahoma Press.

Office of Federal Acknowledgement

> 2005. Technical Assistance Letter to Petition 84A. Department of the Interior. Published online at: http://www.bia.gov/ WhoWeAre/AS-IA/OFA/ADCList/ActivePetitions.htm.

Officer, James E.
    1971. The American Indian and Federal Policy. In *The American Indian in Urban Society*. Jack O. Waddell and O. Michael Watson, eds. 4-65. Boston: Little, Brown and Company.
OHCHR, Office of the United Nations High Commissioner for Human Rights
    2008. United Nations Development Group Guidelines on Indigenous Peoples' Issues. United Nations. http://www2.ohchr.org/english/issues/indigenous/docs/guidelines.pdf.
Orange County California Genealogical Society
    1969. *Saddleback Ancestors.* The Orange County California Genealogical Society. Santa Ana: Aladdin Litho and Art.
Orange County Historical Society
    2010. "A Timeline of Orange County History," electronic resource, www.orangecountyhistory.org/Timeline.html. adapted from Orange County, The Golden Promise, Pamela Hallan-Gibson, 2002, American Historical Press.
Oswalt, Wendell H.
    1988. *This Land Was Theirs: A Study of North American Indians.* Mountain View, CA: Mayfield Publishing Company.
Pevar, Stephen L.
    1992. The Rights of Indians and Tribes: The Basic ACLU Guide to *Indian and Tribal Rights.* Carbondale, IL: Southern Illinois University Press.
Phillips, George Harwood
    1997. *Indians and Indian Agents: The Origins of the Reservations System in California*, 1849-1852. Norman: University of Oklahoma Press.
    1875. *Chiefs and Challengers: Indian Resistance and Cooperation in Southern California.* Berkeley: University of California Press.
Pony Boy, GaWaNi
    1998. *Horse, Follow Closely: Native American Horsemanship.* Irvine, CA.: Bowtie Press.
Robinson, Alfred, trans.
    1846. *Chinigchinich: A Historical Account of the Origins, Customs, and Traditions of the Indians at the Missionary Establishment of St. Juan Capistrano, Alta California Called the Acagchechemem Nation.* By the Reverend Father Friar Geronimo Boscana. New York: Wiley and Putnam.

Romalis, S. ed.

> 1981. *Childbirth: Alternatives to Medical Control.* Austin: University of Texas Press.

Saunders, Charles Frances, and Father St. John O'Sullivan

> 1930. *Capistrano Nights: Tales of a California Mission Town.* New York: McBride and Company.

Shipek, Florence

> 1987. *Pushed into the Rocks: Southern California Indian Land Tenure 1769-1986.* Lincoln: University of Nebraska Press.

> 1978. History of California Mission Indians. In *California*, edited by R. F. Heizer, Pp. 610-618. *Handbook of North American Indians*, vol. 8, W. C. Sturtevant, general editor, Washington, D.C.: Smithsonian Institution.

Sider, Gerald M.

> 1993. *Lumbee Indian Histories: Race, Ethnicity, and Indian Identity in the Southern United States.* Canada: Cambridge University Press.

Southern California American Indian Health Work Group (SCAI-HWG)

> 1999-2000. Meeting notes of monthly meetings taken by C. Coffman.

Strong, Pauline Turner and Barrik Van Winkle

> 1996. "Indian Blood": Reflections on the Reckoning and Refiguring of Native North American Identity. *Cultural Anthropology* 11(4): 547-576.

Svensson, Frances

> 1979. Imposed Law and the Manipulation of Identity: The American Indian Case. In *The Imposition of Law.* Sandra B. Burman and Barbara E. Harrell-Bond, eds. New York: Academic Press.

Thorton, Russell

> 1987. *American Indian Holocaust and Survival: A Population History Since 1492.* Norman: University of Oklahoma Press.

United Nations

> 2007. United Nations Declaration of the Rights of Indigenous Peoples. Adopted by the General Assembly 13 September 2007.